Twenty-five years of child study

Twenty-five years of child study

The Development of the Programme
and Review of the Research

at

THE INSTITUTE OF CHILD STUDY

UNIVERSITY OF TORONTO

1926-1951

by

the staff of the Institute
under an editorial committee

of

KARL S. BERNHARDT, MARGARET I. FLETCHER, FRANCES L. JOHNSON,
DOROTHY A. MILLICHAMP and MARY L. NORTHWAY (chairman)

UNIVERSITY OF TORONTO PRESS : 1951

COPYRIGHT CANADA, 1951
UNIVERSITY OF TORONTO PRESS
REPRINTED 2017
ISBN 978-1-4875-9193-9 (PAPER)
LONDON: GEOFFREY CUMBERLEGE
OXFORD UNIVERSITY PRESS

to

WILLIAM E. BLATZ, M.A., M.B., PH.D.

Director

THE INSTITUTE OF CHILD STUDY
UNIVERSITY OF TORONTO

Foreword

THE CONTRIBUTION OF
CHILD STUDY TO THE UNIVERSITY

IN the modern university with its many divisions and complicated structure, it is becoming more and more difficult to realize the ideal of the university as a community of teachers and scholars. Specialization, and the pressing demands for professional training—to mention but two factors—can lead to isolation, so that the university is in danger of becoming a loose collection of separate, self-sufficient units. Yet, if the university is to preserve its real character, if it is to be an organism and not merely an organization we must be constantly on our guard against the forces which tend to destroy its unity.

The large modern university has found one invaluable way of overcoming this tendency. An important area of study is removed from any rigid departmental or faculty pattern and is made the subject of a free and diverse approach. The Institute of Child Study is such an experiment—the first in the University of Toronto's history. It has long since passed out of the experimental stage, and it has become a model, not only in this institution but in other Canadian universities, of what an Institute should be and what it can do.

If, then, I were asked to say what has been the main contribution of Child Study to the university, I would answer: "It has helped to make the ideal of the university as a community of scholars a reality." Few divisions within the university have so many strong inter-departmental and inter-disciplinary relationships. The Institute has given added strength and direction to its parent discipline of Psychology. It has drawn upon other departments for specialized knowledge. At the same time, it has placed in perspective and has illuminated some of the problems peculiar to other disciplines, as, for example, Psychiatry, Nursing, Dentistry, Occupational Therapy and Education. It has, indeed, been a co-ordinating and unifying force within the university.

But the influence of the Institute of Child Study has not been confined to the university. Child Study is not simply an affair of the classroom and the seminar; it is the major subject on the domestic curriculum of every parent. At all times, the Institute has been aware of the large and eager student body in the homes of the city and of the province. By its programme of parent education, it has transformed the abstractions of research into wise counsels for home and school. As Child Study in the university has helped to fashion an academic community, it has immeasurably enlarged the boundaries of that community.

At twenty-five years of age the Institute has attained maturity, and it is now recognized as a full-fledged member of the academic family. Zealous for its own progress, it is jealous for the welfare of the university. *Maneat, crescat, floreat!*

SIDNEY E. SMITH

Office of the President
University of Toronto
May, 1951

Preface

THIS is the first book of the Institute to be published without the Director's knowledge. It is *for* him, rather than *by* him. Yet in one sense he himself has created it, for the activities of the Institute during the twenty-five years have been instigated, expanded, and encouraged by the vision and faith of the Director. That his staff has presumed to compile a history of his Institute without consulting him is evidence of the initiative he has expected and the confidence he has instilled in those who work with him. That his many friends, including parents of Nursery School children, students, graduates, and colleagues enthusiastically gave their financial, moral, and technical support to the project demonstrates the loyalty and affection with which Dr. Blatz is regarded by all those who know him.

Some time ago Dr. Blatz expressed a wish that the past research of the Institute be published. Because neither opportunity nor inspiration was available, the idea was allowed to lapse. When the twenty-fifth anniversary began to loom on the horizon, discussion among the staff came to centre around the question of how the occasion might be suitably marked. After careful consideration, a staff meeting was held at which it was moved by Miss Fletcher, seconded by Mrs. Johnson, and unanimously passed, that "the research of the Institute be compiled, published, and presented to Dr. Blatz, and that parents and students be asked to contribute to the financing of this venture." After a survey of the research it was obvious that to give it a true perspective it should be prefaced with a description of the organization, and that in order to focus this in true vision an account of the Director who had guided it through its first twenty-five years was not only appropriate but necessary. So the book emerged with both academic and secretarial staff giving much of their time voluntarily, and with each person contributing to the aspects he or she knew best.

The response of the "parents" group was enthusiastic and encouraging. They organized a general committee that assumed all the financial responsibility and consulted with the editorial group on many details of publication. Perhaps their greatest contribution was their complete faith in the staff's judgment regarding content and expression.

The book will of course be of interest to everyone who knows the Institute or its Director. It will also be of value, we believe, to all centres of child study, which will find it a handbook of research papers in this field. To those in the social sciences it will serve as an illustration of the growth and organization of an institution peculiar to the twentieth century and specific in its formulated purposes.

On an occasion such as this it would be all too easy to rush into laudatory phrases and to commend ourselves, our Director, and one another on our past efforts. Such has not been our aim. Rather we have attempted to be as honest, in this volume, as we have insisted we should be in our scientific researches. We have tried, indeed, to tell the truth. "Truth is such a rare thing, it is delightful to tell it." We have expected the author of each chapter to give an accurate picture of the topic as he or she evaluates it; our editing has been minimal because we believe that it is through the unique slants of the individual writers we attain a true vision of the whole. Nothing is here but that which we believe; the significance of the project has been "in the fulfilling rather than the fulfillment."

There is much that the editorial committee should acknowledge in co-operation and help from all those associated with the enterprise. Parents, staff, colleagues, graduates, students, secretaries, and friends have each "played a good part in a great scheme." Only two acknowledgements will be mentioned. Our thanks go to our Director for keeping his eyes and ears tactfully closed and never once enquiring what his staff "was up to," and our appreciation to our secretary, Mary McKeown, who has carried the greatest share of the work and has made the publication of this book possible by incessantly reminding us of deadlines.

The activities of the past provide us with hope for the future. This attempt to solidify our previous efforts has led us to reaffirm our belief that to increase human understanding is the most satisfying of all possible enterprises.

M. L. N.

Institute of Child Study
University of Toronto
June, 1951

Acknowledgments

PERMISSION has been graciously extended by Messrs. William Morrow & Company, Inc., New York, for inclusion in this volume of passages from the following works of Dr. Blatz, *Hostages to Peace, The Management of Young Children, Parents and the Pre-School Child,* and *Understanding the Young Child.* Messrs. Clarke, Irwin & Company Limited, Toronto, and the University of London Press Ltd., London, England, have kindly consented to the reprinting of passages from *Understanding the Young Child.* Messrs. Longmans, Green & Company, publishers of *Mysticism and Logic,* by Bertrand Russell, have given their kind permission for reproduction of an extract from that book.

Contents

The Director

William E. Blatz

A Prophet Not Without Honour[1]

THE CONTRIBUTION OF
WILLIAM E. BLATZ TO CHILD STUDY

Life is a continuous process and there is no one goal or
incentive, other than the desire to learn, which can satisfy
an individual in such a manner that he will not feel it
necessary to interfere in any way with the satisfactions of
others. Learning is intimate and need never be competitive.
A complete life is never finished.

W. E. BLATZ, *Hostages to Peace*

Life is not fulfillment, but fulfilling.
W. E. BLATZ, *Understanding the Young Child*

KARL S. BERNHARDT[2]

A PROPHET is a wise man whose vision penetrates the customs,
thinking, and knowledge of his day to new and deeper meanings.
A true prophet tries to communicate his visions to people, to
share his insight, and thus help to lead his contemporaries to
improved living. Such a man is Dr. W. E. Blatz. Like most
prophets he has been misunderstood, but unlike most prophets
he has had, among his contemporaries, far more followers than
enemies. Dr. Blatz will probably be surprised at the designation
"prophet," just as he has often been surprised to find that some
people are so tradition-bound in their thinking that they have
been unable to catch his vision.

Like all prophets, Dr. Blatz has a biography which should be
sketched briefly. He was the youngest of nine children in a

[1]This chapter appears also in the special anniversary issue of *The Bulletin
of the Institute of Child Study*, number 50.
[2]Karl S. Bernhardt, Ph.D. is assistant director of the Institute, Professor of
Psychology, and recently President of the Canadian Psychological Association.

Hamilton, Ontario, home in which he developed a strong sense of family. He hurried through his elementary and secondary education and arrived at the University of Toronto at a very early age. He breezed through his undergraduate Arts course, making many friends and having no difficulty with such trivia as examinations. His zeal for knowledge about man directed his energies into such activities as demonstrating in Physiology, becoming a member of the Hart House re-education research team, and taking the course in Medicine at Toronto and a post-graduate course in Psychology for the Ph.D. at Chicago. With three degrees from Toronto and one from Chicago, Dr. Blatz was now ready for worlds to conquer. Fortunately for Toronto and for Canada, Dr. C. M. Hincks and Professor Bott were at this time planning a research centre for child development. So Dr. Blatz blithely turned his back on more tempting offers from places in the United States and jumped into the unknown possi-bilities of a nursery school development and an Assistant Pro-fessorship at Toronto. This was in 1924. Within a few short years Dr. Blatz was Professor of Psychology and Director of St. George's School (later the Institute of Child Study). From that day Dr. Blatz has not looked back, nor has he been tempted by the many offers of greater opportunities to abandon his goal of a great Canadian centre of research and training in child development.

Dr. Blatz's almost limitless energies have been directed into many activities but all have contributed to his main objective—to produce, through an understanding of child development and training, a better world. He has a deep faith in goodness and justice. And he believes that through training and education the potentialities in man for happy and effective living can be developed.

Any sketch of the areas of work to which Dr. Blatz has given his time and energies is bound to be incomplete, but the follow-ing will at least illustrate the breadth of his activities. The centre of his activities has been for twenty-five years the Nursery School. As Director, he has been successful in attracting staff who poured their energies into the School, often with very little financial return but always with a zeal for the ideas of the Director. The loyalty of his staff down through the years is a sincere tribute to the leadership of Dr. Blatz. Many generations of students have passed through the school and all have caught some of the vision and optimism of the Director for improvement in methods of child training in home, school, and community.

The "Regal Road" research project in which Dr. Blatz worked for several years provided an opportunity to gather much data on development of the school age child. Here, as elsewhere, he gave more than he received and many parents and teachers can testify to his friendly and helpful advice. Perhaps this—that he invariably gives more than he gets—is Dr. Blatz's most outstanding characteristic; it is a characteristic common to all who are truly great.

The opportunity to widen his school activities came when Dr. Blatz was invited to become Director of Windy Ridge School. Here he put his ideas of educational methods to the test in kindergarten and primary grades, and Windy Ridge became another centre for study and demonstration of advanced ideas of child training and education.

Juvenile and Family Courts claimed some of Dr. Blatz's time and talents in 1927, and he has continued through the years to inject something of his philosophy into the methods of dealing with the bewildered, confused, and misdirected people who pass in endless procession through these courts. Here, again, hundreds of parents have benefited from his clinical insight and helpful advice. Countless families have had the understanding and help from Dr. Blatz that provided the knowledge and direction necessary to change bitterness and conflict to hope and the beginning of effective living.

The famous Canadian quintuplets offered a challenge for both research and service that Dr. Blatz was prompt to accept. He assembled a committee of prominent scientists and organized a research programme in addition to planning the facilities for the routine care and training of the five sisters. Although this

study continued only until the girls were three years old, much
of value had been recorded and accomplished in the early training of the quintuplets.

During the Second World War, Dr. Blatz's contribution
became increasingly significant. He put the facilities of his
Institute at the disposal of the Committee for British Overseas
Children. He gave scores of lectures to Canadian Army officers
on morale both in Canada and overseas. But probably his greatest
contribution was the establishment of the Garrison Lane Nursery
Training Centre in Birmingham, England. At Garrison Lane
hundreds of British women were trained for the important tasks
involved in looking after the thousands of young children
evacuated from the large cities, and others whose mothers were
at work. Dr. Blatz took to England for this task some of his
faithful Institute staff. This work has had an important influence
on the development of Infant Schools in Great Britain.

No account of Dr. Blatz's activities would be complete without mention of the multitude of people who have listened to his
lectures and read his books and articles. For over twenty-five
years both undergraduate and graduate students from various
faculties and schools of the University of Toronto have gained
new insight into child development and human behaviour from
Professor Blatz. His reputation as one of the most interesting and
stimulating lecturers in the University is well deserved. And his
influence on student thinking has not been restricted to Toronto,
since he has participated in summer school courses in a large
number of other centres in Canada and the United States.

Dr. Blatz has contributed to scores of important conferences
on child development and related fields. Through such contacts
he has influenced the direction of thought and research in child
study to an important extent. But his activities have not been
restricted to universities and professional groups. Many tens of
thousands of parents and teachers have been stimulated through
hearing his lectures to think more adequately about their problems of child training and guidance. His sphere of influence has
been widened by his books and articles. These have been read

with interest and profit by people in many parts of the world.

As a physician Dr. Blatz has his own extensive clinical work. Through the years he has treated a great variety of psychological difficulties ranging from problems of child training to adult mental illnesses. This work has given width and depth to his understanding of human living, and through it he has come to affirm the importance of childhood in the development of adult mental health. This has led to his increased study of the ways and means by which children may be rightly cared for and guided to promote their future well-being.

To attempt to evaluate objectively a contemporary is a difficult and perhaps an impossible task. When the valuation is made by one who is a former student and a member of his staff as well as a friend, objectivity becomes an impossibility. However, as I have been given this task, I will at least attempt the impossible, and be prepared to accept the consequences.

Dr. Blatz's philosophy of child training has, of course, undergone changes during the last quarter century. But the changes have been mainly in the nature of refinements, expansion, and clarification rather than in the fundamental principles. His system has a definite emphasis on mental hygiene. It is progressive and democratic in that the evaluation of methods of training is based not on a standard of mere adjustment to the world as it is but rather on the contribution an individual can make to a better world in which the welfare of the individual is fundamental. The Blatzian concept of *security*, has a solid foundation not only in knowledge of human nature but in a clear conception of what is good.

Dr. Blatz is usually unimpressed by the ever-changing slogans and surface techniques of the current educational scene. He is ready to examine any new idea no matter what its source, but he never falls in line with a method or idea just because it is popular. His appreciation of Freud's ideas, despite his disagreement with many of them, is a case in point. He will defend one of his own ideas strenuously, not because it is his own but because it is a good idea; at the same time he is ready to accept other people's ideas, if they are good, and to give full credit to the person who produced them.

Dr. Blatz has a genius for disregarding the unimportant and cutting through language to the core of meaning. He seems to be able to resist the slavery of terminology and jargon. This same characteristic is evident in his clinical work, where his ability to see in the confusion of behaviour symptoms the core of the difficulty amounts almost to magic. This ability to discover immediately the essential meaning of a situation, whether educational, research, or human relations, makes him seem to be impatient with the details of administrative machinery. He sees so clearly what is important that he has difficulty in appreciating the slow process of meandering through the maze of relatively non-essential details which characterizes much of our present-day world.

The opposition, difficulties, misunderstanding, and even ridicule, which Dr. Blatz met in the early years of his work, and still meets but with decreasing frequency, might have caused a lesser man to give up. But Dr. Blatz has maintained a strong faith in child study and in the worth of his ideas, which has led him to persist and to throw more energy into the task of expanding nursery schools, parent education, and improved educational methods. Through the years he has had the kind of security which has enabled him to accept the consequences of his work, whether opposition or praise.

A strong thread running through the complex genius that is Dr. Blatz is a warmth of feeling that colours all his activities and relationships. He values his friends, of whom he has legion. He is intensely loyal to these friends, and they return this loyalty. This warmth of feeling for people is frequently hidden by an outward abruptness which can be disconcerting and misleading. The slowness with which the world accepted his ideas has led Dr. Blatz on occasion to try to shock people out of their complacency; at times this has tended to obscure the essential warmth of personality characteristic of the Bill Blatz his friends know.

We must leave a more adequate evaluation of the work and person of Dr. Blatz for later generations; partly because the true worth of his ideas and influence will be seen in its completeness only when more and more children profit from the influence of his ideas through more adequate education in home, school, and community. This is but an interim report and expression of appreciation, written at the time we celebrate twenty-five years of history of the structure that Dr. Blatz built. "A prophet is not without honour save in his own country." But Dr. Blatz is a prophet who is not without honour *even* in his own city. It is a fitting tribute to Dr. Blatz that the study of Canadian psychology submitted to the recent Royal Commission on the Arts, Letters and Sciences states: "It is no accident that Canada was a very real pioneer in the field of scientific child study nor that it enjoys an international reputation in this regard."[3]

[3]William Line, "Psychology, "*Royal Commission Studies: A Selection of Essays Prepared for the Royal Commission on National Development in the Arts, Letters and Sciences.* Ottawa, 1951, p. 156.

The Programme

Founding of the Institute of Child Study[1]

It has been a fascinating experience to have participated in the beginning of a movement which is wholly constructive; in which the future has far more hope of fulfillment than the past. A good deal of the land has been cleared. There has been some rather erratic plowing; some seeds have fallen, *fortunately,* on barren ground; some few will survive to bring forth fruit. The next quarter century will be a period of consolidation for the great harvest of the succeeding centuries.

W. E. BLATZ, *Bulletin of the Institute,* No. 50, 1951

E. A. BOTT[2]

WHEN one looks back at developments in fields of physical science, one's attention naturally turns to outstanding discoveries or achievements that promise to revolutionize existing ideas or to improve current practices. Such highlights of progress are often associated with circumstances of national emergency, or the ravages of some dread disease, which threaten large numbers of persons. The importance to physics, for example, of radar, with its applications for defence and communications, or of the discovery of insulin and of cortisone to medicine, is readily appreciated, and this appreciation stimulates further scientific effort and public support. By contrast, discoveries in the social sciences are much less dramatic; their development is relatively slow and their acceptance may meet with psychological indiffer-

[1]This article was written for the anniversary number of *The Bulletin,* and is reproduced herein with the author's permission.

[2]E. A. Bott, O.B.E., B.A., is Professor of Psychology and Head of the Department of Psychology at the University of Toronto. He was instrumental in establishing the Institute and took an active part in its administration for the first twelve years.

ence and even opposition. Where there is no widespread feeling of concern, inertia and resistance to change may be expected. These were the circumstances that attended the discovery of the normal healthy young child as an object for scientific study in the early decades of the twentieth century.

This is not to say that the pre-school child was not considered important. He was all-important to his parents and relatives, but unless he was ill, malformed, mentally deficient, or very unusual in his growth or conduct, he was in no sense an object for scientific study. Nor was the child-parent relationship in the pre-school years a matter for methodical investigation. The Church and the State, of course, had interests in the well-being of every child from birth. But no trained workers had the ordinary young child as an object of scientific interest, at least until he entered school and his formal education began. Even then, serious study of the individual as a person rarely began until a later stage when the personality was taking particular shape in adolescence or beyond, and then only when special difficulties concerning his development were encountered. Juvenile delinquency, for example, was a new field, and psychological studies in general were predominantly concerned with post-adolescent or adult subjects, even though psychologists agreed that there were individual differences and that the learning process extended longitudinally through the whole span of life. And although formal education dealt with all the children of public school age and paediatrics dealt efficiently with those who required medical attention, the purpose in those professions was not primarily to understand the child as a person and the parent-child relationships during the pre-school years.

Again, in clinical studies with adult subjects, although the causes of mental disturbance or of misbehaviour at the older level were often attributed to the earlier experiences or circumstances of childhood, surprisingly little was undertaken or suggested towards studying young children directly. Scientifically, there was obvious need, of course, for positive factual support of this backward view of causation, which was speculatively affirmed, by a forward-looking empirical plan for studying young children as they are and as they develop for good or ill.

Such a programme would necessarily involve not only the children but their parents, too, and also a specially trained staff and a suitable laboratory-nursery for the day-attendance of nursery children and parent groups. The idea of a school for child study thus meant providing for the indoor and outdoor activities of a well-conducted nursery and for procedures of parent education, of instruction and conferences with parent groups whose children were of nursery age or older. This conception meant a nursery project with a three-fold purpose, namely, service to pre-school children, scientific study of child-parent relations, and the training of workers for conducting nursery schools and parent-education groups. This conception was a development of the first quarter of the twentieth century in America. It is a university responsibility not merely because of the many university departments interested in the complexities of studying the whole child, but also because of the training provided for undergraduate and post-graduate personnel interestd in this field.

The first Child Study Laboratory in America was begun at the State University of Iowa in 1911 through the vision and efforts of the late Dean Carl E. Seashore and his associates. This pioneer experiment was so successful and convincing that several leading universities undertook similar beginnings in that decade or the next, for example, California, Minnesota, Harvard, Yale, Columbia. Private foundations that had long been concerned with the advancement of science in regard to human development, medicine, and education, also became interested in the normal child. The First World War temporarily interrupted the movement towards child study, but at the same time it intensified the interest in psychological studies that dealt not only with war veterans but with the development of individuals longitudinally through the whole span of life; and it showed also the need for trained personnel who understood the needs of children whose homes were disrupted.

The major advance of child study in Canada came only after the war of 1914-1918, and was in large part an outgrowth of the re-education methods and psychological principles that were developed for the muscle-function training of crippled veterans at the University of Toronto during 1916-1919, namely, that a patient must not remain passive and psychologically dependent, but must become a participant learner, if he is to master his present limitations and thus be able to meet later situations with confidence. In the case of children, the age was earlier and the tasks simpler than with veteran patients, but the motivation with emphasis on self-direction and progressive achievement was similar in the two undertakings.

The potential leadership to pioneer in this new field was not wanting locally. Having contributed greatly in the re-education programme for veterans, the present Director of the Institute of Child Study saw also its broader implications. He readily grasped the idea, first, that these same principles should apply in dealing with persons through all stages of life, and second, that the early stages of this learning process should be the most basic period for study and application. To prepare himself for this broader field of endeavour he planned immediately to complete his medical degree here (having an honours M.A.), and then to take his Ph.D. in basic psychology under Carr at the University of Chicago, which he did in 1924.

At about the same time, through the Canadian National Committee for Mental Hygiene, the support of the Rockefeller Foundation was secured for a five-year grant for the study of mental hygiene problems in public school children in Toronto, and of the Laura Spelman Rockefeller Memorial for a project for the study of pre-school children in the university. Dr. Blatz returned from Chicago to take part in these projects and assumed the Directorship of St. George's School for Child Study, which was opened during the academic year 1925-1926 in a renovated private house at 47 St. George Street. From the beginning this experiment was organized in two sections, a Nursery School Division and a Parent Education Division, each with a separate staff under the Director. It operated at first on a Rockefeller Memorial Grant and under the general sponsorship of the University Department of Psychology, with a management committee on which several university departments were represented. Five years later, under a further grant, the School was moved to larger quarters, which it still occupies, at 96-98 St. George Street. In 1938 St. George's School was taken into the university and became administratively distinct from the Department of Psychology. It thus became the Institute of Child Study, an independent unit under the University of Toronto, in charge of a Committee of the Senate on which are represented the faculties or departments that are mainly concerned.

In the twenty-five years that have passed since child study thus began in our midst, this project has contributed notably to the advancement of knowledge and practice in this field throughout Canada, in Great Britain (during the war-time evacuation of children), and in pace with current advances elsewhere. Its promise of further achievement in the decades to come should be assured.

The Organization of the Institute and Its Place in the Community

The chief aim of education is the development of human
values which will contribute to, rather than make demands
upon, community life.

W. E. BLATZ, *Hostages to Peace*

DOROTHY A. MILLICHAMP[1]

THE Institute of Child Study was the first, and is as yet the only,
organization of its kind in Canada. When it was opened twenty-
five years ago there was no precedent to determine how it could
best serve in its community; no public demand to be met; no
niche in the professional world into which it fitted. It has had
to find and to fashion its role in the community, among the professions, and within the field of science. The field of child study
itself was relatively new when the Institute was organized;
indeed it was one of the first four centres of child study on this
continent. Thus the story of the Institute's growth is a single
thread in the broader history of child study. In choosing to review
the history of the Institute at this time, there is no suggestion
that either child study or the Institute has arrived at any mile-
stone in progress or production other than that culturally defined
as important because it marks the passing of a quarter of a
century. This review is not an attempt to rationalize past errors
nor to forecast future achievements. It marks a pause, even as
activities move forward, to take stock of present effort for
interest's sake and to establish a starting point from which new
endeavours may be undertaken.

[1]Dorothy Millichamp, M.A., has been Assistant Director of the Institute for
twenty years. She was Secretary for the Wartime Nurseries in the Ontario
Government Department of Welfare during the war years.

Throughout the vicissitudes of its growth, the Institute has maintained a single purpose, to study children, in order to contribute valid knowledge to those seeking greater understanding of the children for whom they are responsible. It has striven to maintain its scientific integrity in the whirl of ideas about children, and to work consistently toward its ever-expanding goal.

ORGANIZATION

Today, the Institute has a four-fold function. It contributes to child study through the maintenance of a research programme in child development; it contributes to childhood education and guidance through a demonstration programme in nursery education; it provides the community with leadership in parent education; and it contributes professionally to the field of children's work through a student-training programme. These divisions of activity are not discrete. The Institute believes that theory and practice in child guidance must be continually dovetailed. In its plan of organization these divisions are interrelated so that each is essential to the other and each plays a particular part through which it contributes to the overall scheme. This unity of effort rises out of a common philosophy that determines the general direction of investigation, interpretation, and application. The Research Division is occupied in the investigation of certain hypotheses for which the Nursery School and Parent Education provide observational settings. The Nursery School, as well as being the laboratory, becomes the testing ground for theory and principle. It translates these into methods of practice, puts these methods to use in the Nursery School, and if proven, passes them on to the Parent Education. The Parent Education Division studies the known facts about children and their management, searching out what is valuable for the use of parents. Sympathetic to the practical problems of child upbringing, parent education is alert to discrepancies between theory and practice. So ideas lead to research study, thence to theories of child development followed by the formation of principles of child guidance, and finally result in suggested methods of care, education, and management. The circuit is completed with a return to new hypotheses and further problems to be investigated.

Student training has been made an integral part of the Institute plan. Groups are small enough that students can participate in real problems of child study. They act as part of the Nursery School assistant staff and work on parent education material. For the Institute, student training is a testing ground for ideas and for practices in child guidance. In the teaching of child guidance principles in the community, much depends upon conveying knowledge and establishing a point of view about children. How to achieve these objectives is still a matter of experimentation. Student teaching is the laboratory for trying out methods of presentation and instruction.

The Research, Nursery School, and Parent Education divisions have each a staff whose first responsibility is to maintain the programme of that division.[2] However, a strict separation of duties is avoided. Members of the Parent Education and Research staff take part in the Nursery School programme as assistants; Nursery School and Research staff participate in Parent Education extension work and all members of staff become research observers. The Director controls the overall scheme of investigation and with two assistant directors is in consultation with the four divisions. This general staff of three acts to co-ordinate thinking and progressive effort.

It is an unwritten policy of the Institute that each staff member at some time should receive training experience in the Nursery School, and that every member participate thereafter to some extent. In this role the Nursery School becomes the hub of the Institute. Its very presence in the building is a constant reminder that child study concerns real children in a real world. A second such policy is that all members of staff participate in student training.

THE NURSERY SCHOOL

The children of the Nursery School are considered to be the most important people at the Institute. They are frequently

[2]Four members in the Research Division; four in the Nursery School and five (part-time) in Parent Education.

registered at birth, and they enter between the ages of two and two and a half years and remain until their fifth birthday. They represent a very "normal" group of human individuals, selected to the extent that their parents possess a thoughtful interest in child upbringing. It is this interest which has made possible much of the work of the Institute. The children's parents are asked to attend parent education groups and to participate in research projects while the children are in attendance at the school and after they have "graduated." In many cases two, three, or four children of a family have attended the Nursery School in turn. To date approximately three hundred and fifty families have contributed to the accumulating knowledge of how children live and grow, and the Institute is in close touch not only with the thirty-five children of its Nursery School but with over two hundred children and adults ranging in age from five to twenty-seven years, who have attended in the past. The Institute is in touch with these persons each year as a part of the central research project on child development. In return for their help and co-operation they and their families are offered all consultation and guidance services available in and through the Institute. Speculation about children is realistic under such circumstances!

PARENT EDUCATION

Like Nursery Education, the Parent Education division has its own workshop for study and application. At present five courses are offered yearly to the public, dealing with the following topics: the pre-school, school age, and adolescent periods of development, discipline, and family living. Approximately twenty-five fathers and mothers attend each group. The only selective factor in becoming a member of the group is the interest of the parent who chooses to enrol. In a number of cases the parents attend the courses in sequence as their children grow older.

The aim of parent education is to help the parents achieve greater insight into their children's development and into their role as parents. Parents, like the students, are invited to participate in the field of child study; to think from the known facts to the principles of guidance arising out of these. They are helped to visualize the adjustments in their own approach that such knowledge may imply but are made increasingly aware that there is no simple formula for child upbringing. The groups, from the Institute point of view, provide a laboratory for testing methods of parent education. The problem of successful arrangement and presentation of material is under constant scrutiny. Parents' real concerns are a recurring challenge to theory and principle.

THE INFLUENCE IN THE COMMUNITY

Through its relationships with the families of nursery school children and by its programme of parent education the Institute's efforts are carried far into the community. However, a more specialized form of contribution comes through the programme of student education.

The main student body at present consists of students registered in the Diploma Course in Child Study. This was established in 1944 and consists of a year's training for students who have graduated from the universities or other professional fields. It provides for specialization in nursery education or parent education. Its aim is to provide throughout the community a senior personnel who understand something of the facts, the theories, and the applications in these two fields particularly, and in children's work generally. The Institute is concerned that its students should be able to view facts objectively, should realize the need to relate fact and theory, and should be sceptical of practices with children that are not based on fundamental information. It is hopeful that its students will depend on principles rather than act on dictated practices; that they will thus be able to readapt theory and principle to meet the variety of specialized situations in child guidance. Finally, the Institute attempts so to prepare its students that they will be able to select wisely in following new trends in child guidance. For these reasons the Diploma Course includes, for both groups, the basic subjects of child development, mental hygiene, and research, as well as nursery school education and parent education.

That the above goals have been achieved to some extent is proven by the variety of work which graduates are carrying out at present, namely, work with cerebral palsied, deaf, and blind children; work in mental health clinics, in education, in child and infant welfare; in hospitals; in day care; as well as work in nursery schools and day nurseries and in a variety of parent education settings. A broad understanding of children obtained through experience with them, and the ability to adapt this understanding to a particular child's circumstances, have been the prime factors in the success of these ventures. Added, of course, has been special training where such was available.

In addition to training its own student group, the Institute provides child study for certain academic and professional training courses, namely, Kindergarten-Primary Specialists in Education, Occupational Therapy, and the School of Nursing of the University, and for the graduate division of the Department of Psychology. It also gives lay leader training in parent education and participates in training for assistants in the nursery school and day nursery field. In these courses the content of child study is adapted for application in the fields represented, but always the stress is placed upon understanding, based on knowledge of principles with realization of the need for thoughtful adaptation. Thus the growing knowledge about children is being carried into the community, for use and demonstration by those who will be working directly with children and their parents.

The Institute has the opportunity of participating directly in many of the community undertakings carried on by its graduates, and brings home from these new hypotheses to be put to the crucial test of scientific inspection. But its community contacts do not end with its students. Since children and childhood are a concern of each and every person, and since the Institute's job is to think about children, its staff is called upon to consult with all manner of persons who carry responsibilities concerning children: governing authorities; welfare organizations; people in education, in recreation, and in religion. Its staff members are asked to speak at board meetings, church clubs, parent gatherings, and young people's congregations. Parents from everywhere bring their many problems to the Institute for understanding, and a steady stream of visitors arrives, each with his own special interest in childhood.

THE ROLE OF THE INSTITUTE TODAY

Thus, in the twenty-five years, the Institute has become a resource centre for the community. Child study has brought new vision into children's work and has created its own demand. It has undoubtedly been responsible for bringing adults to a steadily increasing awareness of their responsibility for children's experiences and of the seriousness of their own impact upon the child's personality. It has opened the minds of parents and teachers and all workers with children to a host of new possibilities in attainment of worthwhile goals. It has turned work among children from a humdrum and often seemingly thankless job into perhaps the most creative of all work. In so doing it has, however, increased its own responsibility. Adults, today, have a tremendous concern for children, but their values are diverse and confused. As a result a new hazard faces children. Adults are doubtful of their skill in child management and no longer quite sure of their role in children's lives, so that they are all too ready to grasp at interpretations and practices without fully understanding their sources and implications. While this insecurity is a signal of progress, adult education is becoming increasingly necessary. Child study, like other sciences, is creating powerful tools, the possibilities and limitations of which must be fully understood. Training and maturity and careful judgment are required for their use.

Such considerations suggest that a child study centre of today has a role of leadership as well as a contributory part to play in its community. It must be on the one hand, the depository of information about children from all sources in the field of child study, on the other, the agent responsible for collecting, sorting, and interpreting data objectively, and finally advising in the light of its own particular wisdom. The Institute has its own system of child guidance growing out of a philosophy of human development and based on known facts about human behaviour. This system results from the Institute's effort to integrate the data about children which come to it from many sources; it weighs the information and tries to present accurately the findings of child study to the community in the light of its own evaluation. The Institute reserves the privilege of investigating new ideas and practices before it approves them as ready for use. Where a problem is in an area of child study that is still largely unexplored, the Institute prefers to leave the matter to the adult's best judgment rather than to give a stamp of reliability to partially thought-out theories. In these ways the Institute, as a child study centre, becomes a buffer between the unfinished thoughts of a new field and the children of its community.

At other times, and in the light of information sufficiently proven, the Institute takes its stand in the interest of the children. It then presents the facts relentlessly, well aware that much of what it proposes goes against tradition, culture, and adult attitudes, and infringes upon the grounds of well-established professions.

Child study asks a great deal of the adult world because each adult has his own ideas, ideals, and feelings about children and each community its own traditional practices. To assume new goals, new values, and new ways requires considerable adjustment in a matter so personal as children; it also necessitates courage and some discomfort. In giving leadership of thought, it is a part of the role of a child study centre to understand this final step in the process of child study that begins in the laboratory and ends with the community. It would be possible, and is all too easy, to popularize new ideas about children on the basis of adult foibles. Children are one of our greatest weaknesses, and a play upon our feelings towards them brings a quick response. The adjustment which comes through knowledge and insight is slow and often difficult but it assures judgment and wisdom, and children deserve the best of both.

Goals and Growth
of Nursery Education

Today the nursery school must be looked upon not as
a charitable institution, nor as an expedient for increasing
the number of mothers in industry, nor as a convenience
for parents, but rather as a necessary adjunct to child
care and training. There are many aids—the doctor, the
dentist, the social-service worker—who assist parents to
carry out their responsibilities; the nursery school is an
additional aid for helping the mother and father to prepare their children for a democratic way of living. The
nursery school is for neither the privileged nor the underprivileged, but for both. The nursery school is not a
luxury, it is a necessity.

W. E. BLATZ, *Understanding the Young Child*[1]

DOROTHY A. MILLICHAMP
AND MARGARET I. FLETCHER[2]

With the co-operation of D. I. McKENZIE, R. R. KEITH, E. C. BROWN,
M. L. KIRKPATRICK, C. MAGDER, and M. M. D. WOOD

NURSERY schools are the outgrowth of child study. They came
into being at the time when the human sciences were beginning
to speculate upon the significance of childhood experience for
human adjustment. The concept of development was taking
shape and investigation was reaching back into the early experiences of the adult. Developmental hypotheses could be verified
only through the study of real children and this required an
observational setting. Furthermore, speculation had already suggested new approaches in guidance at the early age levels, which

[1]Reprinted by permission of the publishers, University of London Press Ltd.,
London, England; Clarke, Irwin & Company Limited, Toronto; and William
Morrow & Company, Inc., New York.
[2]Miss Fletcher is the principal of the Nursery School, with which she has
been associated for twenty-four years.

awaited testing. The nursery school was originally established in answer to these needs. As a result, the goals of the nursery school were and still remain those of child study, and the doctrines of nursery education, which have gradually developed, are based upon the theories arising out of scientific study. Now, although nursery education has become a part of education and child care in the community, it remains rooted in child study, is sensitive to each new scientific advance, and reflects the influence of scientific controversy.

Historically, nursery schools have become incorporated as a part of the organized care of the young child which began with the Infant Schools of England. In the expansion of education they followed the kindergarten as a further step down in the age level for which the school takes responsibility. To these established systems the nursery school brings its unique contribution arising from its close association with child study. It is the first organization to achieve a truly child-centred philosophy —a philosophy which considers the child's experiences first and cultural expectations second. The ideal of child-centred planning is, of course, not new. The actual fulfilment of this ideal has had to await the insight which child study is still providing, and nursery schools were the first outcome of that new-found knowledge. Nursery schools represent a positive, mental hygiene approach in child guidance. Based on the concept of development, their aim is to provide for early adjustment and so to open the way for continuing growth towards maturity.

THE NURSERY SCHOOL AT THE INSTITUTE OF CHILD STUDY

The story of the Nursery School of the Institute of Child Study describes how, in one centre, study and research were gradually translated into a doctrine of nursery education. St. George's School was set up in 1926 through the efforts of the Canadian National Committee for Mental Hygiene. Its purpose was to study children. It was placed in the precincts of the University of Toronto, and was operated by an Advisory University Committee on Child Study. This committee consisted of representatives from the Department of Psychology in the

Faculty of Arts, the Faculty of Medicine, the Ontario College of Education, and the Department of Psychiatry. The first and continuing Director was a member of the staff of the Psychology Department. The school was under the immediate guidance of the Department of Paediatrics and the Public Health Department. Research was carried out by the Departments of Psychology and Anatomy. A programme of Parent Education was introduced in conjunction with the Nursery School.

Such was the setting of St. George's Nursery School. Its objectives lay in mental hygiene; its foundation was the human sciences; its professional status was university level; its educational associates were teacher-training organizations; and its students were parents. Surely this would appear to be an overly impressive inauguration for a school of fourteen children, of from two to four years of age. The significance of the event lies in the importance thus attributed to the study of the child and to matters of childhood education and guidance.

GROWTH TOWARDS THE GOALS OF NURSERY EDUCATION

When St. George's School started, goals were specified, but there was little knowledge of the best means of accomplishing these. The Director, writing in 1926, stated the case: "A special technique for dealing with this age has to be evolved. In the meantime the children are enjoying an atmosphere of freedom, self-dependence, regulated habits, adequate social contacts— and of serenity. The latter is the sine qua non of any well-conducted Nursery School."[2] These goals have not altered but it has taken the Institute twenty-five years of study and practical experience to re-define "freedom," "self-dependence," "regulated habits," "social contacts," and finally "serenity" in terms of childhood meaning. The history of the Nursery School is largely the story of increasing knowledge and deepening understanding of the child, giving rise to growing wisdom in his management.

Gradually a doctrine of nursery education has taken shape. The concept of development formed the cornerstone of this doctrine. Although at the outset little was known about the

2*University of Toronto Monthly*, June, 1926.

stages of development and much less about the process, the idea gave rise to a new point of view. It provided the adult with an attitude of easy acceptance towards the immaturities of childhood. It brought the realization of the many stages of immaturity necessary to the final acquisition of maturity. The urgency to teach as rapidly as possible vanished. The child in the Nursery School was to be allowed to grow as an individual at his own pace, developing as he was ready. How best to foster this developmental progress was a matter to be discovered.

LEARNING IN ROUTINES AND PLAY

As a beginning, the Nursery School philosophy maintained one apparently simple premise, namely, that the child is, above all else, one who learns; in other words, the child has everything to learn. All education, it may be argued, assumes learning. This is true. The philosophy of St. George's School differed from that of traditional education in making learning, per se, the important educational element. The content of learning remained a matter of secondary consideration. This philosophy went a step farther, intimating that the total personality of the child develops only as he learns. So the goal of nursery education at St. George's School from the beginning was to evolve a plan by which to guide the learning of children. Learning was defined simply but dynamically as the response whereby the child seeks to meet his needs within his environment. Thus understood, success in any learning situation becomes the experience of satisfaction following effort, and what behaviour the child learns will depend on what brings satisfaction. The responsibility of the adult is then to make provision for successful learning throughout the child's day. Science has not changed the daily round of a nursery school child's activities. Actually, a comparison of the Nursery School's daily programme of 1926 with that of 1951 shows them to be almost identical. Inevitably, this programme is made up of an assortment of routine and play periods. It has been the part of science to discover what these routines and play mean for learning and development.

In St. George's School, from the beginning, the routines of

the nursery school day were considered to hold a prominent place in the child's learning experience. Here organic needs are fulfilled; so that routines seemed the natural area in which successful learning should begin. Within the nursery school programme, routines were given adequate space and time and the procedures were elaborated to make of each a worthwhile experience in effort, satisfaction, and success. Consistency of routine programme was maintained in order that the child would attain an efficient, fully satisfying habit. Individual differences were studied to assure satisfaction for each child. Research observation has verified the value for mental hygiene of such effective learning in the routines of life. Practical experience has proven that the young child enjoys a worthwhile routine that is taken seriously by both himself and the adult. Latterly it has been shown that routines properly arranged provide for experience in self-dependence and responsibility, in sound adult-child relationships, and in "security." Therefore, the Nursery School of the Institute has continued to give routines a place of importance in the young child's experience.

The significance of play in the young child's learning was in the beginning largely based on assumption. Development seemingly took place, but the process was unknown. The early Nursery School programme simply provided the child with every known opportunity in the form of materials for play and children to play with, and gave him time and freedom to do his own learning in answer to his own needs. Gradually, through research observation, areas of learning began to emerge. Play with things was separated from play with other children. Research showed that in dealing with his material world the child gradually developed a pattern of self-initiated purposeful and attentive activity, attended by increasing exploration and experimentation as ability increased. In brief, he became "interested." This interested activity became one of the developmental goals of the Nursery School programme.

A part of the child's play time was designated primarily for learning with materials. Distractions were kept at a minimum and social stimulation indirectly controlled by providing for individual occupation. The child was encouraged to determine his own choice of material and what he should do with it. The adult role was one of interest but limited interference. Through observation, certain materials were demonstrated to have greater value for fostering interested activity. Criteria for judging the value of play materials have been formed in terms of opportunity for activity, variety of use, progressive use, and creative possibilities. In this period of play, the children present a picture of seriousness and preoccupation, each with his own activity, but with a friendly interest in those of his playfellows. The doctrine of nursery education of the Institute today continues to maintain a balance between social experience and experiences from dealings with the material world.

SOCIAL ACTIVITY

Early observations of the social activity of young children yielded little helpful information about the process of social development. They did, however, show one very significant fact, namely that sociability at the pre-school age is exceedingly immature and progresses rapidly with experience. Such observations verified the hypothesis that social development is a matter of learning, and emphasized the value of the nursery school as an opportunity for such learning. The problem in nursery school practice now became one of determining how the social activities of nursery school could be so limited and simplified that they lay within the limited possibilities of the young learner.

Since every moment of a nursery school day is essentially social, to some degree it was necessary to consider each situation in the light of its social implications. The procedures throughout the day were rearranged so that only the simplest relationship was required, namely doing what others do, but doing so individually. In other words, group organization was reduced to a minimum. Beyond this minimum was ample opportunity for increased interaction as the child chose to attempt it. In the outdoor play period provision was made for all levels of freely organized group play. At the dinner hour and during music and stories the child was given an opportunity to attempt more difficult social relationships under adult supervision, but no child was ever required to participate socially in these situations. In other routines, and in the indoor play period, social experience was deliberately minimized by making the procedures more individual. Thus relaxation from the need to respond socially was provided and over-stimulation avoided.

The supervisory role of the adult, as originally set out, was that of minimum interference in social free play: "Let the children solve their own social problems." With further enlightenment adult responsibility has been increased. The adult has become adviser and arbitrator, and asserts control when necessary. Her objective in so doing is to simplify or clarify the learning situation for the child and so help him to a satisfactory solution. It is believed that since all the children of a pre-school group are very immature, the experiences that they gain from one another may, if no direction is given, lead to the development of forms of behaviour which will curtail rather than improve co-operative relationships. If security is lacking, aggression or withdrawal are the natural social responses, neither of which furthers positive social learning.

From the beginning, competitive social relationships have been discouraged in the Nursery School and their use avoided as an incentive for learning. This principle is based upon the theory that competition disturbs the normal course of learning by confusing the goals of the child's effort and interfering with more fundamental satisfactions and success. Socially, competition places him in an opposing instead of a co-operative relationship. Arranging an environment free of competition is considered to be very important at the early age levels when the foundations of a sound learning pattern are being established.

Emotional Expression and Control

Another aspect of the child's development considered in the Institute's doctrine of nursery education was that of his emotion.

Emotional control and expression were viewed as problems of learning. As with the other forms of child behaviour, emotional immaturity was expected and accepted. The child was guided gradually towards successful control by the simple device of making little of his outbursts and, when he was ready, recalling his efforts to the situation in hand. Deeper insight was gained when research suggested that emotion functions as an integral part of learning, that is, that it is aroused as the child is moved by his need to search for satisfaction. It became evident that anger and fear reflected the child's learning experiences and occurred when he was unable to meet his needs fully within the situation; or when problems were beyond his grasp or his efforts were hampered; or when he was not succeeding sufficiently to feel confident in his approach to problems. Thus anger and fear were recognized as symptoms of difficulty in the child's life. To guide a child towards emotional stability requires consideration of his total life experiences.

Need for emotional expression has recently received considerable emphasis in the field of child guidance. In early days positive emotions, pleasure, joy, affection, exuberance, were taken for granted but received little study because they were not a matter of practical concern. This aspect of the child's experience is just now coming under research investigation. In the meantime the Institute believes that such emotion is part and parcel of the contentment the child feels as the result of satisfying routines, the enthusiasm arising through his free and successful play with material and other children, and the confidence created from consistent adult guidance.

Thus the curriculum which has emerged in the Nursery School of the Institute as a result of research and nursery school practice is directed towards the development of satisfactory habits, accompanied by experience in responsibility; of a pattern of "interested" activity; of a co-operative approach to other children; and of emotional stability through expression and control. Finally, through learning in all these aspects of experience, the curriculum fosters the development of a learning approach towards life situations; that is, a willingness to expend effort with confidence that a solution can be attained.

DISCIPLINE AND ADULT-CHILD RELATIONSHIPS

With this increasing insight into the child and his experience there has come greater understanding of the role of the adult. The importance of adult-child relationships has received increasing emphasis in the nursery school field. Over the twenty-five years, the Institute has perceived with increasing clarity the dynamic influence which the adult has upon the child's total development as an individual. In the early days of St. George's School the adult's function was stated in gross terms, namely, that she must arrange for the child to receive "a balance of freedom and control." This principle formed the basis of a plan of discipline. It was practised very simply by controlling the action of the children in chosen areas and by withholding control in others. In routines the child was expected to follow directions, in his play he was free to choose his own activities. Later this principle was redefined in terms of the child's learning. The child should learn on the one hand to "conform," on the other to "non-conform."

Conformity meant that the child willingly accepted certain goals and procedures as laid down for him. In the Nursery School a part of the adult's plan of discipline was to establish "requirements" for the child suitable to his needs and ability and to help him to learn how to meet these successfully. If he refused to accept these minimum essentials, it was equally her responsibility to help him to realize his mistake in refusing. It was here that the Nursery School plan of discipline broke most definitely from traditional practices. When the Director announced in 1926 that corporal punishment would never be used in the Nursery School, he was stating a principle that has remained central to the Institute's philosophy. The child must neither be forced nor frightened into acceptance. He must be guided in discovering the value of conformity so that he chooses to conform willingly. It followed that requirements must be worthwhile and just, and that so-called "punishment" should be replaced by simple teaching. Such practices as threatening, blaming, rewarding, became unfitting in the light of this philosophy. "Meaningful" consequences were introduced as the method of teaching the child the outcome of refusing or accepting essential requirements. Such experiences for the child were chosen to be simple, natural, and to hold no fear. From the adult point of view such a method required above all else consistency—consistency of requirement and in the carrying out of teaching consequences. This method of discipline gave rise to a sound relationship between child and adult, since personal feelings of disapproval were out of place and no fear entered into the relationship. It was not an easy rule for adults born in an older tradition. It necessitated in the adult a faith in the concepts of development and learning sufficient to enable him to refrain from personal insistence, in order that the child might have practice in the use of his own judgment.

More recently a further step in clarifying adult-child relationship has been taken. It is now realized that this willing acceptance of conformity on the part of the child is a result of his growing attitude of trust and respect for the adult and her control. In other words, a child receiving consistent careful control develops a "feeling" towards the adults who administer it; this gives rise to a dependent co-operative relationship—a sense of "working together" on jobs to be done. In the Nursery School it has become each adult's responsibility to deal with each child in such a manner that he can gain a confidence in and respect for her. Also, it has become the practice for each staff member to work in all situations and with every child, to help the child develop attitudes of confidence and co-operation towards his adult world as a whole.

There is a second aspect to the adult's role and to her plan of "discipline." The child must also learn the enjoyment and the "art of non-conformity," or so-called creative endeavour. As described above, in the early days of the Nursery School the adult simply "remained in the background" in those situations where freedom was provided. Recently child study has pointed out that to provide freedom is not enough; the child may not accept the freedom offered to him. Whether he explores and experiments, whether he is ingenious and adventurous in discovering the possibilities of his world, depend on his trust in and respect for himself. Thus it is suggested that if he is to conform, the child must believe in others, if he is to be "creative," he must believe in himself. The adult, then, has a double role: first, to foster a sound dependent relationship, and second, to encourage independence. To encourage independence requires a dynamic rather than a passive adult role. The adult must find ways of supporting and encouraging the child in choosing his own goals and investigating ways and means of accomplishment. If she thus expresses respect and trust in his efforts, she gives him a sense of assurance. Gradually he acquires self-confidence.

All of which brings the history of St. George's Nursery School up to date and refers our thinking back to Dr. Blatz's statement of the goals of 1926—the sine qua non of a good nursery school is "serenity." Can this be defined in 1951? Perhaps it can—although one hesitates, knowing that there is a depth to childhood experiences as yet untouched. In the light of twenty-five years of progress at the Institute, it might be suggested that the goal of a nursery school is a group of children who are busily engaged in learning and who have confidence in their adult world and a beginning of trust in themselves so that they are neither restive under restrictions nor afraid to act freely, and whose prevailing feeling is one of enthusiasm—is this perhaps the way to serenity?

NURSERY EDUCATION IN THE COMMUNITY

The St. George Nursery School was far from alone in its endeavours of the past twenty-five years. No more fitting time than the present could be chosen to express sincere appreciation to the students who have contributed their experience and thinking in the growth of the principles and practices of nursery education for which the Institute stands. The first students of St. George's School to go out into the field of nursery education were faced with innumerable difficulties. Training at this time was largely made up of practice. There was little content about which to talk and no ready words in which to express what was being attempted. These students learned by "feel." Thus equipped they faced a sceptical public. The first two nursery schools in the community under the direction of graduates of the Institute were experimental demonstration ventures. With inadequate building facilities and meagre funds these schools were set up to prove the worth of nursery schools for educational purposes. By dint of consistency of philosophy and practice they did. The parents approved and assumed responsibility for maintaining these two schools in their respective communities. These schools are still running and many other such community schools have been established throughout Ontario and in other parts of Canada. It took time for the public to realize that nursery schools are for every pre-school child and not simply a philanthropic provision for the underprivileged. The final step in this direction has recently been taken in Ontario where the provincial government has introduced Junior Kindergartens for three- and four-year-old children into the Public School system.

The early students faced another difficult venture—namely, that of introducing principles of nursery education into the traditional day nursery. These day nurseries had been set up long before the time of nursery education, to give care to the young child whose home life was inadequate. Boards and superintendents realized the need of programme revision and sought help. Provision of full day care presented many problems of child guidance for which there were as yet no ready answers. Students entering this area of work had to maintain a research approach; changes had to be brought about slowly and each step of the way proven.

And then came the challenge of the Dominion-Provincial Wartime Day Nurseries of 1942 to 1945. This project fell directly upon the shoulders of the small experienced group of nursery school workers in the field and in the Institute. Building standards had to be established and buildings found; equipment had to be designed and produced; programmes had to be adapted and experimentally tested. Continuous emergency training taxed field workers and Institute alike. Through the hurry and confusion, the children were never forgotten, nor was the goal of nursery education—serenity. A special tribute is due those who entered the field during this war period. Hurried to their job with foreshortened training, they continued to seek for deeper understanding of the child and of their role and did not stop until they had grasped the philosophy and the goals of nursery education. Again in the Wartime Day Nurseries, consistency of thought and practice prevailed. The parents grew in understanding and approved. They petitioned that such day nurseries be maintained in Ontario and they were. This eventful period in the history of nursery education and the Institute brought about another advance. The Government of Ontario introduced a licensing policy whereby all institutions caring for pre-school children would receive supervision.

It is the Institute's most sincere hope that the doctrine of nursery education for which it stands will continue to grow and change in the future as it has in the past. Then the system will never take precedence over the child.

Activities and Aims
of Parent Education

Most parents are resolved to do the best they can for their children. A conscientious parent, intent upon the task of rearing children, must be moralist, psychologist, educator, philosopher, theologian, physician, nurse, and dietitian, in addition to being a father or mother. This has been for generations the task set for themselves by intelligent, well-intentioned parents. Unassisted, a parent of today, knowing as he does the possibilities of all these contributing factors to his child's future, would be undertaking an almost hopeless task. But there are nowadays many aids to parenthood, even though there are no adequate substitutes for it.

W. E. BLATZ, *Understanding the Young Child*

FRANCES L. JOHNSON [1]

With the co-operation of H. BOTT, N. I. CHANT, A. M. R. FOSTER, M. W. BROWN, K. S. BERNHARDT, and D. M. DOUGLAS

PARENT education has, from the first, been an integral part of the plan of the Institute of Child Study. From the beginning it has been assumed that only with intelligent parent co-operation can optimum results in child training be achieved. When the programme began, parent education was a new field in Canada, lacking both content and leadership. These had to be developed. Mrs. Helen Bott, the first leader, describes the beginnings thus, "A week in New York with the Child Study Association was my formal preparation for this new experiment in education. It was an exciting experience, opening up new vistas of ideas and

[1]Frances Johnson, M.A., has been lecturer in the Parent Education division of the Institute for some twenty years. Since 1947 she has been appointed to train lay leaders in parent education for the Community Programmes Branch, Ontario Department of Education.

experiment. This slight equipment was probably an advantage, for it meant that leader and group were on the same level—we were all learning." Much has happened since then and many changes have taken place.

The programme was initiated with two groups of twenty-five parents. These groups were made up of parents of children in our own Nursery School and of people in the community who were keenly interested in achieving better family relationships through more adequate methods of child training. Mrs. S. N. F. Chant says, "While there may have been a few in these groups who came because parent education was new and intriguing, my recollection of these groups is one of alert, interested, highly intelligent women with a very real interest in the problems and responsibilities of family life. Their leader, while having very limited experience at that time in the field of Parent Education, possessed unusual qualities of heart and mind, and the discussion, under her wise guidance, was always stimulating."

ACTIVITIES

In a very real sense these two groups provided the laboratory of parent education. The members were willing to devote time, not only to attending groups, but to reading, study, and observation in the Nursery School, all of which added to their knowledge, and made the discussion more meaningful and its content better adapted to practical application. The groups were unique, since the discussion was reported verbatim and later studied and discussed by the Parent Education staff with the Director. None of the groups that have met each succeeding year could have received more careful study and attention. These two groups set the pattern that has since been followed, although the methods have varied and have included lecture courses, lectures with discussion, and guided discussion groups.

As the courses continued, the content became more definite. The first course to be organized on a working basis as a result of research was that on the Pre-school Child. It was given as the basic course since that period is first in the life of the child and offers parents the earliest opportunity for training. Other courses subsequently were added: Discipline, the School Age Child, Adolescence, Family Relationships. In the course of time, through continued study and research, Discipline replaced the Pre-School Child as a basic course. As it presents a philosophy of guidance fundamental to all learning, it has become at the present time the foundation on which the content of other courses rests.

With the growth of interest in parent education, a new development took place in response to the needs and demands of the community. There were more registrants than could be taught by the small part-time staff, so, with potential leaders available, a training programme for leaders was developed. In addition to those in the community interested in leadership, members of staffs of social agencies became aware of the possibilities presented by such training and signified their desire to avail themselves of the leadership training course. The students worked with children in clinics, creches, day nurseries, and placement agencies, and realized how much parents needed help in facing and solving problems of child rearing. The staff of the Institute could not hope to cover as many groups as would be required, neither was it desirable that they should do so. They lacked the training in social work and also the close knowledge of the people who would form the personnel of such specialized groups. They could, however, help with content and leadership methods. As a preparation for adapting the material to the needs of the leaders, a staff member led groups in comparable settings, accompanied by a second staff member whose assignment was to record the meeting, what took place, and the material that seemed to cause difficulty in understanding. This was discussed by the staff and adaptations made.

An arrangement was made whereby interested social agencies released certain workers for training one day a week over a two-year period during the academic session. A course was planned that provided a series of morning lectures on content and practice of parent education, observation in the Nursery School, and an

afternoon or evening observation in a parent education group led
by a staff member. Reports giving an analysis of the efficacy of
the material and the reactions of the group were required. In the
second year each student, with the help and supervision of one
member of the Institute staff, led a study group in the social
agency represented. While the training course at this stage was
primarily designed to meet the needs of social agency personnel,
others who were interested in making parent education available
in their neighbourhoods through Home and School and church
groups, were admitted. There were no formal qualifications for
admission but applicants came sponsored by organizations that
would benefit through their training. This course became an
integral part of the Institute programme and laid the foundation
for the present Lay Leadership Training Course and for the
parent education section of the Diploma in Child Study. Of this
first course Mrs. Chant says, "All staff members participated in
it, Nursery School, Parent Education division, as well as the
Director himself, and all found their work and lives enriched by
these contacts in the community."

The close relationship between research and parent training
continued to operate in the new setting of leadership training.
This plan of leadership training continued from the time of its
inception until 1947. The content of courses was changed from
time to time to include new findings in research and in order to
meet the needs of leaders more effectively, as these needs became
evident through close study by the Institute staff and the leaders
themselves, who were encouraged to view their efforts objectively
and to suggest improvements. The personnel changed over the
years to include more people who were interested from the view-
point of the community rather than of social service. So the
training was directed towards providing lay leaders and social
service workers with knowledge that would enable them to help
parents in the practical setting of the home.

In 1947 a new development occurred with the incorporation
of Parent Education as an option in the Diploma for Child Study
Course. The Lay Leader Course was continued and still con-

tinues, but many of those who had taken it wished to have the more intensive training that a graduate course offers. For the first time formal qualifications, a B.A. or equivalent, were required of the registrants. Those taking this course emerge as fully qualified Parent Education Leaders on the professional level.

As an evidence of the growing demand for leadership in parent groups, the Community Programmes Branch, a division of the adult education programme of the Ontario Department of Education, consulted the Institute in 1946 regarding the possibility of conducting lay leadership training groups throughout the province. After a trial period during which several members of staff participated, one member of staff was appointed on loan to the Government to do this work. The plan for training was to conduct training groups in selected centres for one week each year over a period of five years, the courses being given in sequence: Discipline, Pre-School Learning, the School Age Child, Adolescence, and Family Relationships. After the intensive training period, those trained give the material back in their community through the groups which sponsored them. Reports are sent in after each meeting to the Institute where they are carefully examined, and additional help is subsequently given by the Institute where needed. This constitutes further training. Through public demand the training centres have grown, in four years, from four to twenty-four, and some centres have had two courses in one year. With this rapid growth the value of the training is amply demonstrated, although the total impact in communities is difficult to measure.

Aims

The aim of the Institute in its parent education programme has been, and still is, to help parents gain insight through knowledge and understanding into their relationship with their children and with the family as a whole, and to use this insight in the practical field of guidance. The programme endeavours to lead parents to think objectively and adapt principles to the child's

experience so that the child may emerge a responsible adult.
The field of its endeavour covers parent training in all its facets
and has led it into many paths: Parent Education groups, Lay
Leader training, professional leader training, preparation of outlines for use by leaders, pamphlets for use by groups, the publication of books on child training, and a quarterly, *The Bulletin,*
which presents a philosophy of home and family life in relation
to the present-day world. The growth has been towards increasing impact on the community at large and the dissemination of
the results of research for use in families.

Where parent education will go in the future is unpredictable,
just as it has been in the past. The need will direct the effort.
Mrs. Bott has grasped the vision when she says:

It is always more interesting to look forward than to look back. The
challenge of the present compels us to evaluate the parent education movement, not so much in terms of what it has accomplished, as in what it may
offer us in relation to the world we live in, and what it has that may direct
our future. Probably none of us realize how profound are the changes in
our social and economic life over the past few years, or how they are
modifying our family life. Take only such instances as the rising cost of
living and housing shortages, not to mention the overhanging threat of war.
We need to see our homes in the setting of the world situation. Isolationism
in the home is as out of date as isolationism in world politics. To create a
happy home is not enough. We must make our family life bear on those
issues of war and peace which convulse the world today. A new philosophy
of home and family life, set in this context of world affairs, is a first charge
on the parent education movement.

Secondly, the dynamics of human relationships is the focus of interest
for social psychology today. Here parent education could play an important
role. Apart from the fact that the family is the basic pattern of social
relationships, the parent groups themselves provide an interesting field for
the study of social interactions. Here one can observe the clash of ideas
and personalities, the emergence of leaders, the resolving of differences,
the development of thinking, and the integration of thought and action that
are all part of the process of the successful group. Beside adding to the knowledge of the research student there could hardly help but be a carry over
into home situations of the skills gained from such an experience. To be able
to reconcile conflicting wills, to know how to find unity of thought and
action, to be creative in our relationships with one another in the family
is to produce something of value which the home can expel through its
members to ease the tensions of our industrial and public life.

Lastly, I would suggest that nothing is more needed today than a
study of leadership. Our civilization stands on the brink of ruin by reason

of dominant leadership based on the power principle. A leadership that inspires and integrates rather than compels is the great need of the world. Such leaders inspire intelligent and willing followers. The emergence of leadership trends from nursery school onwards is a fascinating field for investigation, and an essential for training. This applies, of course, pre-eminently in the home where the great problem of parents is how to guide and direct, so that the child learns to govern himself. This is the essence of our democratic way of life—often more honoured in the breach than in the observance. Its pursuit and practice is probably the greatest contribution that parents can make in saving civilization.[2]

[2]From an article that will be published in *The Bulletin of the Institute of Child Study*, 1951, No. 50.

The Research

The Research

Human beings cannot, of course, wholly transcend human
nature; something subjective, if only the interest that
determines the direction of our attention, must remain in
all our thought. But scientific philosophy comes nearer to
objectivity than any other human pursuit, and thus repre-
sents, though as yet only in a nascent condition, a higher
form of thought than any pre-scientific belief or imagination, and, like every approach to self-transcendence, it
brings with it a rich reward in increase of scope and
breadth and comprehension.

BERTRAND RUSSELL, Mysticism and Logic

MARY L. NORTHWAY

With the co-operation of D. A. MILLICHAMP, H. SHEPHERD, J. G.
PARTRIDGE, P. KARAL, B. M. TALBOT, and M. R. McKEOWN

THIS is the story of the growth of the research at the Institute
of Child Study from its inception to the present.

The most accurate account of this research can be obtained
by reading the seventy-six theses, seventeen monographs, three
articles, and eleven books which it has produced; abstracts and
summaries of these immediately follow this dissertation. By
perusing these the reader will be quite able to form his own
review. As we have already read the original documents in considerable detail it would seem not entirely impertinent to preface
the abstracts with our own impressions. These we have organized
into four parts: influences on the research of the Institute; its
growth and development; its present projects, and an appraisal
of what it has achieved. That our outlook has been somewhat
parochial is a result of the fact that on this occasion we have
limited our observations to our own past efforts. That our efforts
are only a small part of the general child study movement is
demonstrated in every thesis and publication. One needs only

to look up the bibliography each quotes to be convinced of the many strands from which our own particular material is woven.

This review has been restricted to the studies and publications of the Institute actually completed. It has, however, included all of these regardless of their merit and by doing so bares its total self to public scrutiny. This review is not a scientific document so much as an historical one. And its value is not so much in the reports of the actual studies as in the fact that they reflect the growth and a process of development of a research programme. The psychologically trained reader may well turn the skills he has used to examine the growth of a personality to understand the growth and development of this programme and to evaluate the structure of the research which has resulted from it.

The programme need not apologize for its inadequacies by stating that it, as most other research programmes, was carried out amid budget limitations, administrative pressures, and war responsibilities. These may indeed have contributed to, rather than distracted from it. We are not concerned with describing what our programme should or might have been; we have found the task of discovering honestly what it has been, exacting enough.

INFLUENCES ON THE RESEARCH

General. Research in child study has been influenced by clinical psychiatry, by scientific method particularly as adapted to academic psychology, and by the characteristics of psychologists who have specialized in this area.

Freud's discoveries made it impossible to postpone serious study of the child. His pronouncements on the importance of early childhood he fortunately substantiated with such extraordinary embellishments that public interest was attracted. This created in certain quarters at least a strong incentive to conduct studies to prove him wrong. Among enlightened medical and psychological people, however, the significance of the early years

became accepted as the clue to the secret of both mental pathology and the idiosyncracies of human personality. Doctors and
psychologists accepted Freud's emphasis on childhood but
doubted his evidence. Indeed, to the person with scientific
training data from psychiatric sources seem at worst distorted
and at best limited. Psychiatric information regarding childhood
has been obtained retrospectively from sick adults and these
accounts inevitably are reflections of the peculiarities of the
memory process itself and of the particular colouring the illness
gave to the patient's introspections.

However, the stories woven by the clinicians seemed to be
formed from the real warp and woof of human living and
appeared to interpret human dynamics rather more vividly than
did the reports issuing from formal psychological laboratories.
In these, since at least the time of Wundt, it had been demonstrated that the principles of scientific method could be used
with a high degree of accuracy in the study of human beings.
The accepted findings on the esthesiometric index, the relation
of stimulus and response, the laws of colour vision, substantiated
the belief of psychologists in the efficacy of scientific method and
encouraged them to hope that by such an approach they would
one day achieve discoveries equal to those already achieved in
the areas of the physical and biological sciences. That the discoveries of the laboratory were for the most part completely
isolated from the human being in action concerned no one, least
of all the laboratory psychologists. Their satisfactions lay in the
triumph of subjecting their problems to observation and sub-
mitting their data to measurement.

The understanding obtained from clinical insights and the
facts discovered from scientific method are reconciled largely
through the characteristics of many of the individuals entering
the field of the human sciences, and by the role defined for them
by the community. Many students join these disciplines because,
as they somewhat naïvely state, they "are very interested in
people." Indeed, interest tests reveal that they score highly on

humanitarian, social service, and literary interests and relatively low in mathematics and science. Although their subsequent training in scientific thinking develops a high degree of objectivity, by it such interests become directed and controlled, rather than stultified.

As soon as his professional life begins the psychologist is given a role in the community in which he is expected to guide the action of human beings, or, at least, inform others how to do so. Often this guidance is requested in areas about which the psychologist has little strictly scientific information. For example the illustrious William James became the preceptor of countless college students through his dissertations on habit, and became the interpreter of the spiritual life through his discourses on the Varieties of Religious Experience, although even he had little scientific evidence for what he said about either.

So throughout the years the community has demanded much from the psychologist and he has attempted despite the inadequacies of his scientific progress to assume responsibility for meeting its needs. In terms of the above qualities a psychologist may be described as a humanitarian at heart, a scientist by training, and a counsellor through the role society has thrust upon him. Thus he may find self-expression most fully in an environment which permits the pursuit of knowledge of human development and encourages its use towards the increase of human welfare. One such permissive environment is child study.

Child study reflects the formal influences of both psychoanalysis and scientific psychology. It also reflects the vital influences of the personalities who have guided it. Yet child study is not psycho-analysis or psychology or welfare service. It is a new discipline, the purpose of which is to gain knowledge of children's development and to interpret this understanding into the wisdom of practical use. Its research has required that while scientific principles be held inviolate, scientific method be adapted to this discipline's new subject matter, the lively child. It has had to recast the technique of the *ivory-lab* into forms suitable to the home, the playground, and the school. And particularly it has had to seek the final verification of its discoveries neither in the reliability of its statistics nor the validity of its consistencies, but in the application of these discoveries to all those situations in which children live and move and have their being.

Local. The research at the Institute of Child Study is a reflection of the pattern of the 1920's pervading such institutions on the continent. Its purpose was based in a humanitarian spirit, its subject matter became the child as he developed in his life settings, its approach the integrity of the scientific method. All child centres contain these three ingredients; their differences are in the proportions and the organization with which they are blended.

The particular *environment* in which research has grown at the Institute has influenced its particular pattern. The Institute has been deeply imbued with belief in the scientific method and at the same time responsive, perhaps overly responsive, to the needs of the community. From the beginning it has been both a research and an educative centre. Much of its research has been instigated by practical problems and its results directed to practical fields. During its first five years, while the leaders of dignified society were projecting their bewilderment of this novel organization by berating it, the Institute had already produced two books for parents (B1 and B2)[1], co-operated in consultations and researches with the public school system (A1), the juvenile court (T3), the Children's Aid Society (T1), the Infants' Homes (T4, T5), and the Ontario Mental Hospitals (T8). The demands of the community for immediate help in all phases of children's welfare far exceeded the available supply of service.

On the other hand, the Institute's close association with the

[1]The letters and numbers given in brackets refer to the index of the documents presented in the next section. These documents are given chronologically by the year of completion. T denotes an unpublished thesis, A an article, M a monograph, and B a book. Documents in each category are numbered in chronological order by year, and within the year alphabetically by the author's name.

University departments, particularly that of Psychology,[2] established high standards of scientific integrity. Because of this, the
problems for study were selected on the basis of whether they
could adequately be dealt with by scientific techniques. "Two
essentials in collecting information will be to deal with points
that are unambiguously recordable and if possible quantitatively
measureable." (M1) These studies at first were limited to observations of children's overt recordable behaviour (M1, T2, T6,
T7, T9, T10) and these in themselves presented difficulties
enough!

The Institute might be pictured as a warehouse meeting the
public's requests for goods insofar as it could obtain good stock
from its research supplies, but refusing to fill orders with shoddy
stuffs, stamped with the trademark of science merely to satisfy
a customer or build pseudo-goodwill relationships. Its scientific
standards have made its programme slow but solid, while its
humanitarian concern has kept its research realistic. These
qualities in 1926 gave rise to the epithet "radical" and in the
1940's to the taunt "reactionary." Through the years, however,
they have kept the work consistent and prevented it from being
concerned with short-term goods demanded by the rise of some
over-popularized intangible psychological fad. The Institute has
not, therefore, expended its energies on creating esoteric products suitable for weapons in use in the academicians' battle of
wits but useless in the market-places of human life.

Certain factors of the Institute itself also influenced the research. One of these is the fact that the Institute supervises its

[2]The head of the Department of Psychology, Professor E. A. Bott, was instrumental in establishing the Institute and has remained its close colleague. The
administrative relation of St. George's School and the Department of Psychology
during the early days has perseverated in close association through the years. In
fact the Director and the Assistant Directors are also members of the Psychology
Department's staff at present. Researches towards M.A.s and Ph.D.s conducted at
the Institute are accepted by the Department of Psychology for presentation to
the School of Graduate Studies. In spite of many associations with other departments these facts have influenced the Institute's research towards being predominantly psychological in nature. Other aspects of child study, physical growth,
health, anthropological, and cultural factors have been considered only to a
relatively slight extent.

own Nursery School. The School is an integral part of the Institute, sheltered under the same roof, and since the early days under the direction of one staff. Designed as a research centre, it has been used directly for at least thirty of the studies. But it has become also a testing ground in which the results of research can be applied; the judgment of their *validity* being made on the basis—is this possible, practical, and natural in the daily living of the normal pre-school child? Too, because of the nursery workers' familiarity with young children, research apparatus and procedures have been carefully designed to be meaningful to the child. Puppet shows, puzzles, xylophones, story books (for example, see T17, T22, T29, T32, T51, T57, T68), have been incorporated not only to meet scientific criteria but to be presented as an interesting and relevant part of life for the young child. They form a pleasant contrast with some of the materials now available for psychological work with children, which reflect more fully the ideational content of the mental hospital than the freshness of the young child's world.

Another influence is that the Institute staff apparently stay a long time and are all very busy. The Institute has been under the same director since it began and several of the staff members have retained their appointments almost as long.[3] This has given a continuity to both thought and organization and one study has developed from another more from the continuity of interest than because of a strictly logical sequence. There are, however, no members of staff devoting their full time to research.[4] Nearly all members of the Institute hold other appointments or undertake outside duties. Since members of staff are engaged in work other than research, this results in a breadth of interest on one hand, but a minimum of research produced at a senior level, on the other.

[3]The length of time certain members have been on the staff is as follows: Assistant Directors—Miss Millichamp, 20 years; Dr. Bernhardt, 15 years; Nursery School—Miss Fletcher, 24 years; Parent Education—Mrs. Bott, 12 years; Mrs. Chant, 17 years; Mrs. Johnson, 23 years; Research—Miss Shepherd, 12 years.

[4]Although seven members of the Institute staff devote some of their time to research, the total amount of staff time given to research at present is the equivalent of that of 2.3 full-time research persons.

Complementary, however, to the staff situation is the fact that a great deal of research has been produced by students working with vigour and enthusiasm at the M.A. level. In many centres the M.A. is considered merely an exercise in research. However, the abstracts in this book demonstrate that although the M.A. provides opportunity for practice in research methods, the specific studies undertaken may be chosen within a general continuing project and may equally well contribute to the development of that project. The influences of this staff-student situation have been to develop a research programme in which the progress is consistent, the projects creative.

In summary, then, it may be said that while the Institute, like all child study centres, reflects the influences of both clinical and scientific interests in children, its particular research programme is coloured by its own external relations both to the community and within the university, and by its internal organization in which its Nursery School forms the hub of the universe and its staff provides both continuity of thought and extensibility of interests.

The Growth of the Research

Method. The research of the Institute begins with observation of habits and is presently concerned with studies of security. As in all science, the underlying problem has been the discovery of method and each particular study, regardless of its actual results, has furthered this search by claiming an added area within the territory of scientific principles. In 1951 it is difficult to realize that twenty-five years ago there were few means available for studying children in their natural habitat. It is only when introducing naïve students to the Nursery School and asking them what they plan to investigate that we realize that knowledge of *what* to observe is a sophisticated accomplishment. Too, it is only when we set them the task of, for example, recording the length of time a child plays with one toy, that we realize that *how* to observe is a complex skill developed through years of training; and it is only when we direct our students to analyse the results of their observations that we remember the complex process by which quantitative and qualitative methods have been derived to meet the data of child study. The student recapitulates in his learning the historical sequence of the quarter century.

Through the accumulated efforts of the investigators methods are now available by which it is possible to observe and to classify children's overt behaviour in such areas as habits (M1, T8, T15, T27, T44); emotion (T10, T13, M4 and M10); play (M1, T30. T76); social relationships (M2, M3, T31, T33, T34, M14, M17, T53, T54, T55); to record children's understanding of a situation (T17, T35, T40, T50, T51, T12, T68); to investigate learning (T2, T29, T32, T52, T57) and attention (T7, T64) and to adapt these methods to a wide range of settings (T8, T11, T21, T36, T44, M12).

Advances in methodology in the general psychological field and other areas have been incorporated into the Institute's research. For example, statisticians have concurrently developed means for dealing with a small number of cases and this advantage is reflected in the more recent researches.

While methods are still lacking by which all aspects of child development may be observed, gradually it has been possible to survey increasingly deeper areas and bring these into the range of scientific scrutiny. What has been accomplished has been done without deviating from the integrity of scientific principles. That the methods can still be improved is obvious, that they have not been adapted as yet to meet all aspects of child activity implies that the Institute will be justified in continuing for another twenty-five years. But such proven methods offer to any investigator a means of discovering how children actually do behave and thereby prevent him from forming erroneous interpretations of normal behaviour or setting up programmes that expect behaviour far different from that manifested by the ordinary child.

If the Institute wished to commend itself for any part of its research, it would certainly not be on the discovery of any miraculous answer to the nature of child development, nor on any flash of brilliancy in the results of its studies, but rather for its continued and often tedious endeavour to develop its investigations only insofar as they could honestly be brought under the objective methods of scientific principles. It has not been that inner personality qualities, feeling, and values have been considered unimportant; rather they have been considered too important to be studied until we can devise *methods* worthy of them. Any other approach would be a regression to pre-scientific speculations and result only in distorted interpretations influenced by errors of human fantasy.

Pure and practical studies. Research efforts have been directed both towards increasing the understanding of child development and towards clarifying practical problems that arose in children's work. These may, for convenience, be termed "pure" and "practical" research. The first two studies made by the Institute, one the cataloguing of children's misdemeanours at a public school (A1) and the other a study of habits and play activities at the Nursery School (M1), illustrate these two trends. An example of practical research, the investigation of misdemeanours was an attempt to analyse the forms of behaviour that violated the requirements of school life, thus causing disturbance to the authorities and perhaps distress in the child himself. The frequency of each type of misdemeanour, the variation over the age range, and the relationship of it to other characteristics of the children were worked out. This was a co-operative undertaking. Teachers participated in the study through keeping records, while the research staff co-operated with the teachers by giving psychological help with difficulties.

In contrast with this, the second study was concerned with habits and was undertaken to discover the basic processes in the psychological development of the young child. Thus it is an example of "pure research," the problem being of scientific rather than immediate practical interest. Observations of amount of sleep, control of elimination, development of eating habits and type of play activity, were observed and compared for different age levels of Nursery School children.

These two studies are the prototypes of those that follow, which also in terms of their primary purpose may be classified as *practical* and *pure* research. Following the pattern set by the two first publications we find that of the first two student theses one was concerned with which are the better risks for adoption, legitimate or illegitimate wards, (T1), and the other, what are the patterns of children's learning and how do these compare with those of the apes? (T2). In the following year one student seeks to discover the criteria for a foster home (T5), another the manifestations of emotion in the young child (T10). Ten years later the energy of the staff was directed to the immediate opportunity of studying the Dionne quintuplets (M12), while a Ph.D candidate analysed the degree to which school children of different ages could understand the concept of consequences (T40). In 1946 one study was devoted to the consideration of playground arrangements in the wartime nurseries (T59), while another was involved with the patterns of learning by which children come to solve problems (T57). Thus, throughout the years, pure and practical research have progressed; studies arising in the practical area being determined mainly by the pressure of an immediate problem and those in the pure field by their place in the sequence of thought and investigation. It is obvious, of course, that in spite of their difference in initial focus, their method and results have intertwined and woven themselves into the total pattern.

The development of pure research. Most of the studies of child development can be classified under the following topics: activities in routines and play; learning; emotion; experience; social; analysis of the developmental process and security. Chart I lists each study under these topics and beside the year in which it was produced. This can be read to show the order in which the studies were completed and the extent of effort in each area.

Chart I should not be read as if the vertical columns form a direct sequence. Actually the lines of influence would be horizontal, vertical, and diagonal. That is, a study under Play may not be directly influenced by the previous study listed under

CHART I

STUDIES IN "PURE" RESEARCH ARRANGED BY YEAR UNDER THE
MAIN TOPIC OF INVESTIGATION

Year	*Routines & Play*	*Learning & Discipline*	*Emotion*	*Experience*	*Social*	*Developmental*	*Security*	*Year*
1926								1926
1927								1927
1928	M1	M1						1928
1929			T2					1929
1930	T6, T9	T7	T10					1930
1931			T11					1931
1932	T15	T14	T13	T12				1932
1933	T19			T17	T16, M2			1933
1934		T22			M3			1934
1935	T27	T30	T28, T29		T31			1935
1936			T32	M8				1936
1937			M10	T35	T33, T34			1937
1938		T44	T42	T39, T40	T37	T43		1938
1939	T48		T45		T46, T49			1939
1940			T52	T50, T51	M14		M15	1940
1941								1941
1942					T53			1942
1943					T54			1943
1944					T55			1944
1945				T56				1945
1946			T57		A3, M16	T58		1946
1947					M17	T61		1947
1948		T63		T62				1948
1949				T68	T69	T65	T66, T67	1949
1950		T76			T72		T70, T71, T73, T74, T75	1950

Play but rather its impetus may be given from a problem raised by a study in learning. For example, T63 (1948), a study of children's attention in play, does not grow out of the immediately preceding study in this area (T30). Rather, it arises from a problem under Development and is a longitudinal study of the growth of attention through the nursery years.

It should also be noted that investigations in one area have not been terminated either because all is known or because interest has waned. Indeed "routines" for which no study is recorded since 1939 are again the basis of certain studies connected with present investigations of security; and both learning and emotion will regain a new life in the social, developmental, and security studies.

The chart should be used only as a guide; otherwise it gives an erroneous impression. The growth of the research may better be considered a vital rather than mechanical process. It may be likened to the life process itself in which each event is reformed from what precedes and reorganized into its place in the future whole.

The order in which the studies developed is no random sequence. Gross classification of behaviour as it occurred in routines and play had to be undertaken before studies of learning could profitably be commenced. For learning is not a directly observable process but an inference made to account for change in observable behaviour. Similarly, studies of the particular forms of behaviour termed "emotion" arose as a natural outgrowth from the cruder general classification.

Studies of experience and social activity awaited an advance in observational method before their complexity could be investigated. And studies of the life development of children obviously had to remain quiescent until the children had time to develop.

Studies of security were reached as a culmination of all the previous research and are an attempt to integrate in a new whole the various aspects of child behaviour that had been dealt with in part in the earlier analyses.

The development of these various topics and their interrelationship will become clarified as we consider in the next section the progress in each.

Sequence of the studies

STUDIES OF ROUTINE AND PLAY. Although studies of routines and play were undertaken first because of the adaptability of these activities to scientific observation, accurate knowledge of them is important as a foundation for understanding child development. The life curriculum of the young child is made up almost completely of routines and play. How he learns to meet adult-designed situations in the routines is the basis for the processes of his later formalized learning and his willingness to deal with established social requirements. On the other hand, how he learns to handle the situations in which he is free to determine his own goal (play) is the basis for his development of creativity, initiative, and social participation. By observing the initial processes of human learning in these two great areas of requirements and freedom the fundamentals of the process itself are revealed and the factors which distort, thwart, or disturb that process may be discovered in their incipient forms.

Studies of routine and play began in 1928 with observations of nursery school children's activities in sleeping, eating, elimination, and play (M1). Thereafter, studies in play and routines were separated. Routines and habits included studies of children's initial activities in adjusting to nursery school (T6), of non-useful habits, tics (T9), of resistance to conforming to routines (T15), of food preferences (T19), and eating habits (T27), and of the degree to which children take responsibility for carrying through the routine (T48).

In play such questions were considered as the length of time pre-school children attended in a play project (T7), differences in paintings by children of different ages (T14), the ability of children to reproduce music (T22), and the interests of children in play materials (T30). Two recent studies have approached the topic from new angles—the growth of attentive adjustment of pre-school children (T63) and individual differences in children's painting (T76). The first of these (T63) is concerned with the development of attention and interest in the same child over a period of eighteen months; the other (T76) is an attempt to evaluate the validity of the prevalent interpretations of personality symbolism in children's painting.

For students of personality the area of the routines offers particular interest. As these are established to take care of the child's basic biological needs, the organization of his physiological appetites (A2) is formed around them. The organization of the psycho-physiological life provides the foundation on which the edifice of personality structure is erected. Thus, while routines are made for children and not children for routines, the knowledge of how to arrange routines properly in terms of children's needs and abilities is the first channel for influencing sound personality development.

Early play activity also has importance for personality organization. Many clinicians believe that a child's personality is most fully expressed in play. Although some of the interpretations of play therapists and projectivists seem to be based on assumptions rather far removed from observable facts of the normal child, it is undoubtedly true that in play the child expresses his interests freely and thereby learns the essentials of creativity, inventiveness, and self-direction.

STUDIES OF LEARNING. As soon as children's behaviour is observed it is found that the observed data vary with various factors of the children. For example a child of two plays alone sifting the sand, a child of four joins his playmates in building a sand castle. How to account for this change is a problem of great concern to the psychologist. He infers there is some process of change *in* the child; this process he identifies as "development," if it seems to occur merely because of the passage of time he classifies it as "maturation"; if it occurs as the result of the effort expressed during the interval it is called "learning." Learning is assumed but not defined in the early publications of the Institute.[5] It appears to be interpreted as *directional change* of activity brought about through experimentation with the environment. Thus learning is placed in the realm of measurement both on the basis of amount and of direction of change. To effect this change in the desired direction a procedure, called at first a plan of training or control and later a plan of discipline, is advocated. "Discipline is always a plan of teaching and not a scheme of punishment."[6]

[5]Preliminary statements of this are given in B1, p. 280f; B2, p. 215f and 291f; B3, p. 32f, but a systematic statement does not appear until B8.
[6]B5, p. 126.

The first study of learning (T2) consisted of observing the series of activities that young children used to solve problems. The problems selected were approximations of those described by Köhler in his studies of apes. The detailed protocols of the children's activities show the individuality of patterns used in reaching the solution successfully. This variation of process by which desired learning is achieved by different individuals is of fundamental importance both for a theory of learning and for practical education. The way a person learns is as significant as what he learns. The topic was touched again (T57) but has not been further extended.

Certain factors influencing learning have been investigated in different studies. The influence of various factors on learning have been studied. The amount of *instruction* given in progressive schools is much less both in school hours and instructional periods than the amount given by public schools. Yet by testing on standardized tests of "tool" subjects it was found progressive school pupils had learned as much as comparable children at public schools (T28). In the experiments of learning mirror drawing (T29), and in solving a problem (T57), it was found that direct instruction had little or no favourable effect. These studies substantiate the Institute's emphasis on planning conditions for the child's learning rather than teaching him by direct instruction.

The influence of *imitation* was shown (T52) to accelerate learning when the child was allowed to watch children only slightly older and more skilled than himself.

Failure was shown to be detrimental to learning (T32) and if it were continuous its adverse effect increased. The author is careful to distinguish error and failure, and by failure implies the type of response evoked by well-known frustration experiments— that is, the problem was designed to be unsolvable in spite of the child's best efforts. In the Institute's general discussion of learning, failure (in the sense of error), is considered to be an essential part of learning, but failure meaning complete discouragement with the task is incapacitating.

A group of studies (T8, T11, T40, and T44) demonstrate

that the Institute's theory of discipline is pragmatically valid. Blatz derived and expanded his theory of discipline from Carr's[7] theory of sensory consequences. He believes learning is facilitated if the environment is kept constant so that any action is followed by a consistent consequence. Thus an action always produces the same result and therefore is deleted from or fixated in the individual's repertoire depending on the desirability of the result. In the Institute's own studies this has never been validated by *experimental* evidence. That the plan works, however, is shown by the *pragmatic* evidence, namely that in a school (T40), an institution for the mentally defective (T8), and in homes T11, T44) in which the plan of discipline is used, children learn the patterns of activity desired.

STUDIES OF EMOTION. Emotion is given a place of prominence in modern psychology, possibly because of its complex manifestations in personality disorders. At the adult level its intricate influences and obscure expression make it difficult to observe and to interpret. The young child, however, is much more likely to express his emotion directly through either explosive behaviour such as crying, hitting, and stamping, or in restricted behaviour in sulking, leaving the situation, or rigidity. In the young child emotional episodes can therefore be observed and when they are analysed appear to arise when the child is incapable of dealing with a situation and by some factor in the environment or himself is prevented from continuing to try, that is, when his learning is thwarted.

Four studies catalogue the forms of emotion and the conditions giving rise to them in nursery school children (T10, T45), infants (T13), and children of school age (M10). The first of these (T10) designed forms by which emotional behaviour could be recorded. The study of infants (T13) discusses the nature of emotion, considering that it is the behaviour that arises in a situation for which the individual has no adequate response and in which his attempt to find one (learning) is thwarted so that

[7]Harvey A. Carr, *Psychology, a Study of Mental Activity* (New York: Longmans, 1925), 432.

he attacks more violently or withdraws from it. A later study investigated milder emotional expression (T45). The observation of older children (M10) extends these principles to show that with increased learning there is less non-adaptive emotional behaviour and links this fact with a plea for a plan of discipline that provides adequate learning situations rather than one that merely punishes chaotic emotional behaviour.

Two studies (M8, T42) consider the form of positive emotion expressed in laughter. The first, a study of nursery school children's episodes of laughter, results in the suggestion that laughter arises with a resolution of conflict; the second demonstrates the influence of the social situation in facilitating emotional expression in laughter.

STUDIES OF EXPERIENCE. Although its studies began with observations of gross behaviour, the Institute never belonged to the behaviouristic school. It ignored the psychoanalytic unconscious because this concept by definition was outside the bounds of scientific observation, but, unlike the behaviourists, it emphasized consciousness. It assumed that the individual not only moved in the world but was aware of it. His awareness or experience, however, could be inferred only from his expression through behaviour in motor or verbal form. Studies of the child's inner experience began in 1932. Some of these have shown considerable ingenuity in the methods used for obtaining an expression of the child's thought. For instance, in one study (T17), a puppet show depicting an adult and child in nursery situations was used to obtain children's interpretations of "right" and "wrong" actions. To discover the extent to which children appreciate consequences of actions, plays were used for younger children (T50) and descriptive situations presented to older ones (T40). From these it was found that nursery school children understand disciplinary consequences (T50), and that this understanding extends to more remote and complicated consequences as the child increases in age (T40). This same study (T40) demonstrates that children at a school in which discipline is based on consistent consequences have more skill in predicting consequences than have children in schools based on other educational philosophies.

One study (T51) investigated children's recalls and modification of story material. This indicated the transformation of literary material in the child's imagination and resulted in practical suggestions for authors of children's books.

In 1932 an investigation was made of children's responses to the Rorschach (T12). The author discovered that if children were scored according to the standard procedure they showed bewildering tendencies to mania or schizophrenia. Although nothing was reported of the study at the time it indicated the dire results which arise from interpreting children's responses on psychological tests according to adult standards. Such adultomorphism has tended to pervade personality studies and only recently has become a cause of concern[8] in the child-clinical field. This study shows that much that is pathological in an adult is normal at some point in the age-scale.

A second study of the Rorschach (T62) was completed in 1948. The hypothesis is that the test can be used with children not as a means of personality diagnosis but as material by which the genetic development of thinking can be studied. Comparing these two studies shows the advance made in method and statistical analysis during the fifteen years.

A recent study (T68) is concerned with the pre-school child's concept of self in his social relationships. The test was carried out by using paper dolls and the child was asked to select the dolls representing himself and other members of his family. The accuracy with which the child selects dolls representing figures in his real family increases with age. The results are such, however, as to suggest that clinically minded adults are inclined to assume that the young child perceives and identifies dolls as his parents or siblings more readily than he really does.

[8]Cf. S. R. Pinneau, "A critique on the articles by Margaret Ribble" (*Child Development*, Vol. 21, No. 4, Dec. 1950).

STUDIES OF SOCIAL DEVELOPMENT. The importance of social interaction is equalled only by the difficulty of studying it. At the time the Institute's research began, social psychology had been concerned mainly with "the herd," cultural patterns, and had only recently attempted to relate social activity as an appendage of behaviourism.

The first attempts of the Institute were, therefore, to develop a method for observing social behaviour of children (M2), and to analyse such observations from a small selected group (M3). In a monograph (M3), the author describes children's activities with materials and other children and shows the relationship of various factors such as age to these. She points out that while the methods used give accurate results, they offer only a partial analysis of personality; this incompleteness, she states, was justified at the time because these activities are amenable to objective observation and their measurement may serve as a basis from which an inquiry into the inner integration of the individual may later be made. The methods formulated served as a basis for further studies such as that of dominant-submissive behaviour (T46), relationships between child and adult (T49), analysis of children's methods of initiating contact (T53), and social contacts among five non-siblings (T33 and T34), and among the Dionne quintuplets (M12).

Another type of inquiry was made (T31) in which 518 public school children were asked individually to name their friends. From the great number of answers the writer's major problem was to find a means of statistical analysis which would describe the complexity of the relationships. In spite of the methodological difficulties some definite findings resulted, including the fact that a child's social relationships extend beyond the limits of any defined group such as the classroom or school situation.

In 1940 Moreno's[9] sociometric techniques were introduced for use in a summer camp and an incipient scoring method estab-

[9] J. L. Moreno, *Who Shall Survive? A new approach to the problem of human interrelations* (Boston: Beacon House Publishing Co., 1934), 435.

lished for them (M14). The use of these with nursery school children and a comparison of the results with those obtained by observation was made in 1944 (T55, A3, M17). The actual contacts and the choice preference complement rather than duplicate one another, giving insight into two aspects of the child's social life.

A study of the constancy of nursery and young school children's social choices (T69) showed that typical social constellations can be found at these levels and that group patterns and friendships remain fairly well stabilized over an eight-week period. Statistical means to handle the data and methods of depicting graphically the predominent relations were worked out.

A study (T72) related sociometric scores with the Rosenzweig picture-frustration test and showed that many factors considered to measure personality differences by reaction to frustration do not differentiate between children of high and low sociometric status. From the factors that do differentiate, it is concluded that children who are highly accepted are less overwhelmed by frustration and more apt to blame others than themselves for the difficulty than are children of low acceptance. It may be that the use of such projective tests along with social or sociometric measurements will provide one key for unlocking the door for studies of personality integration mentioned in earlier publications (M3).

In various areas one isolated investigation appears several years before the problem is studied comprehensively. In the social studies in 1943 (T54), an investigation of the actual play of a child with his chosen companion was compared with the play of the child who had been chosen. This area of investigation of the interaction between children of known social relationship has become the focus of interest for three studies concurrently in process (1951). Suffice it to say such studies depend on the methods of observation and analysis created through the earlier research and on various refinements of sociometric techniques developed over the years. They demonstrate that material considered at one time mystical or intangible can gradually, through accumulated experience, be brought into the area of scientific method.

DEVELOPMENTAL STUDIES. In 1946 an examination was made of the cumulative records which had been kept of children who had attended the Nursery School since the beginning of the Institute (T58). This described the records in use—records of infancy kept by the parents; the regular records of routines, emotion and discipline, and intelligence tests while the child was at nursery school; and records obtained from later annual interviews and tests. The derivation of the forms is described and an evaluation given.

These records, supervised and kept by the senior staff, have formed the crux of the Institute's research on development. Based on normal children, they should provide a clue to understanding of the process of human development. In order to gain a complete picture, analysis of the records has had to wait until a sufficient number of subjects attained maturity. Since forty of the first children are now over eighteen years of age, an analysis of their development will probably become the next major project of the Institute.

Meanwhile, three studies based on the accumulated records have been made. Two (T43, T61) were concerned with the variation in I.Q.'s obtained for the same child at different age levels. Another (T65) analyses the reports on the child's social activities and is essentially an attempt to formulate a method by which the rich amount of recorded information may be organized.

STUDIES OF SECURITY. Security is the term given to that integrative principle of personality mentioned early in the researches and implied in so many of the studies. As has been mentioned, the early studies were observations and classifications of behaviour. The studies of security attempt to discover means by which selected behaviour can be observed as an index of the individual's inner integration.

The first study of security (M15) describes security as "essentially a subjective experience implying a feeling of adequacy to meet future consequences." In two books (B6 and B8) general outlines of the concept are given and it is shown that it arises from the process of learning and the direction of this through discipline. Security is a truly psychological concept in that it is concerned with conscious experience and studies the *phenomenon* reflected from the event. It has an implication for social psychology in its consideration of the importance of human relationships.

The studies include one publication (M15) produced in 1940; this describes a technique for investigating security by questionnaires for adults. The answers are scaled so that security may be measured in familial and non-familial relations. There are also seven M.A. theses which have been completed during the last two years. These for the most part derive scales for measuring security in various areas. They are included in this book by title only.[10] To understand abstracts of these would require more knowledge of the concept than is at present available in accessible form. It is hoped that a full statement will be prepared in the near future and data from the studies made available at that time.

PRESENT PROJECTS

Studies are at present in progress in four main areas of interest. Because each of these is rooted in past research they will be described here, although they more rightly belong to a preview than to a review of the research.

The developmental study.[11] The first children attending the nursery school are now adults and complete records are available of their development. At present the staff is analysing the records of the forty oldest subjects. If the matter of observing and recording was a problem of the early studies, the method of analysing these documents presents an equally baffling problem of today. The material is unique—for forty normal adults are accumulated

[10]Abstracts are available in the Institute's library under Research Index No. 3.
[11]Under the direction of Miss D. A. Millichamp. For the past three years these studies have been assisted by Mental Health Training and Research Grants.

sample observations of their development as it occurred from infancy to the present. These are augmented with results of mental tests given at yearly intervals and complemented with psychological measures taken at the adult level by an examiner unfamiliar with the subject's history.

The staff has constructed forms on which all the data for one individual is organized, and has analysed these for a limited number of subjects. It is anticipated that in another year a monograph describing the study will be produced. The chief contribution of this work will be that it describes the *process* of development based on longitudinal studies of the same individuals from birth to maturity, thereby forming a contrast with present literature which is based largely on age norms attained by the cross-sectional method.

Community studies.[12] The children at the public school (described in A1) in 1925 who served as subjects for the research at that time are now, of course, mature adults. Through the years it has been possible to keep records of many of these individuals and at present two investigations are being conducted: first, a comparison of the individual's adult adjustment with his recorded school behaviour; second, a study of the earlier and subsequent family history of a group of siblings at the school in 1925— records of four generations are now available and will enable an evaluation of heredity and environmental influences to be made.[13]

Social studies.[14] Two main studies are in progress. The first is a longitudinal study of social relationships of nursery school

[12]Under the direction of Dr. Blatz and Miss Helena Shepherd. This study has been financed in part by grants from the Mental Health Training and Research Budget since 1948.

[13]These two studies were not a part of the original research Programme of the Institute; they were undertaken simultaneously by the Director of the Institute, under the auspices of the Toronto Research Committee of the National Committee for Mental Hygiene. In 1933, when this Research Committee discontinued its efforts, these studies were continued from an office in the Institute building with partial financial support from the National Committee for Mental Hygiene and various other funds for several years. By the academic year 1939-1940 they had been included in the Institute research programme and budget.

[14]Under the direction of Miss M. L. Northway.

children from two to four years of age. The second is a study of
the social interaction of children of various ages of known sociometric relationships in a defined situation. An introduction to this
has been made in three theses completed this year. These have
served to clarify methodological difficulties. The present plan is
to adapt the methods of group dynamics to observe children
working through a problem or formulating decisions and to discover how their interaction varies in terms of the age group
observed and the sociometric relationships existing among the
subjects.

Studies of security.[15] At present efforts are being made in
three directions: (1) extension and refinement of the scales to
measure adult security; (2) attempts to obtain measures for
estimating security in the young child; and (3) the development
of a book discussing the philosophy underlying the concept of
security, the psychological processes on which it is based, and
the means by which it can be appraised.

What Has Been Achieved?

It would be easy to criticize the research programme with
regard to both depth and width; the sparcity of studies past the
M.A. has meant that many problems have been left at a rather
superficial level; and the concentration of studies on the nursery
school child of a middle class urban society has narrowed the
range of the knowledge acquired.

Yet to criticize properly requires that some standard or basis
of comparison be available. A basis of comparison is difficult to
find for few, if any, organizations have published a statement of
their total research conducted over a quarter of a century. We are
more familiar with judging programmes of research by reports
containing only the more significant of an organization's efforts.
In this review we have unearthed the whole of the research
endeavour. A more glamorous picture might have resulted had
we featured the "high lights" and based our review on a des-

[15]Under the direction of Dr. W. E. Blatz. These studies have been financed
in part by grants from the Defence Research Board since 1948.

cription of the painstaking early study of children's habits, the
scholarly researches into social behaviour and personality by Mrs.
Bott, the spectacular analysis of the Dionne quintuplets by Dr.
Blatz and others, the brilliant theses, and the present investigations of security. Yet it is doubtful if in this or any organization
the stellar performances could exist other than in the whole
constellation.

Our evaluation will not be that of the critic, but that of the
clinician. The task of the clinician is to appraise the assets and
liabilities of his client—neither to praise nor to condemn, but to
understand. The clinician's evaluation is based not on a set of
absolute standards but rather on the value of his client's goals
and the extent to which through his actions he is approximating
these.

Our evaluation of the research will be based on the following
question:

If the expressed goal of the Institute's programme has been
to adapt scientific procedure to the study of children and thereby
to increase understanding of human development, to what extent
have the activities of the twenty-five years led towards it?

Towards veracity. This review demonstrates that it is possible
to adapt scientific methods to and maintain scientific integrity in
the study of children provided that one has considerable patience
and is unwearied by the required efforts. Continual persistence in
the face of bewilderment and continual vigilance against tempting psuedo-scientific techniques have been necessary. By plod-
ding slowly along the hard road of science and refusing to be
beguiled by the tantalizing will-o'-the-wisps of esoteric mystical
philosophies, explorations have gradually been made charting
increasingly wider areas, and sorties, at least, have been undertaken into the deeper complexities of human development.

That the Institute has not discovered the final meaning of
Truth is not surprising. Problems which have baffled philosophers and theologians for centuries will hardly be solved by
psychologists in twenty-five years. Indeed it is doubtful whether
the human sciences will be any more successful in these en-

deavours than their predecessors have been. They may, at best, reach the realization that the great whys of life are not answerable, but are made more acceptable with the increase of human knowledge.

If the Institute has not achieved the Truth sought by the philosophers, it has adhered to that form of truth which Sir Richard Livingstone terms veracity:

I mean by it that veracity which does its best to tell the truth, the whole truth and nothing but the truth: where it is uncertain, confesses to uncertainty; where it lacks knowledge does not pretend to it; which is candid and frank, takes no unfair advantage in argument, is careful not to misrepresent an opponent or to ignore the strength of his case and the weakness of its own.[16]

By maintaining its constant search for scientific veracity, the Institute has been called *rationalistic*, as if this appellation were derogatory. That it has been rationalistic in its approach is apparent. What else can a scientific centre be? Accepting the fact that inner physiological functions as well as the outer forces of the physical world influence experience, the Institute believes that only as these are translated into consciousness and reflected in behaviour do they become psychological data. It has chosen, therefore, to approach the problem of human living by the rationalistic methods of science, rather than to rely on faith in intuition or philosophical speculation.

That "the human understanding is no dry light . . . for what a man had rather were true he more readily believes," should be known to the psychologist, above all men. For his studies of human nature bring him continual evidence of the peculiar interpretations and distortions that colour the experience of the individual. The psychologist, above all men, must be aware of the need for the use of a corrective lens by which his own experience may be free from his personal distortions. The scientific method provides the best such corrective and by it the psychologist is able to reach, if not truth, at least objectivity.

In historical perspective the research programme has shown

[16]Sir Richard Livingstone, *On Speaking the Truth* (Toronto: University of Toronto Press, 1946).

continuous loyalty to its accepted scientific faith. It has shown that the dry light of science casts an increasingly widening beam, that whereas twenty-five years ago habits could be viewed objectively, at present it is possible to bring the individual's security at least out of the shadows of mysticism. In this progress there lies hope. It encourages the belief that, given time, increasingly wide areas of human affairs will become similarly understood and that the darkness of human destruction and despair will vanish in the light of scientific understanding. Thus "the mists of *accidia* disperse before the light and heat of the sun."[17]

Towards human understanding. The goal of the Institute has never been merely to study children scientifically, but to study them scientifically in order that human understanding may be increased. The various pieces of research are each made of their own particular colour and cloth yet put together they form no haphazard patchwork but rather a patterned tapestry of balanced harmony and design.

Good inferences are as important as accurate observations. And understanding arises not from the data themselves but from the facts created out of them. All the various researches are consistent with the story the Institute creates of human development and many have contributed directly to it. Throughout all this story run two recurring themes, the first, that the individual is a *learning* creature; the second, that he is a sensuous being.

A PHILOSOPHY BASED ON LEARNING. That the child learns is so obvious a fact that it is difficult to realize the width of its implications and that it is possible to form a philosophy of life upon it. It was obvious also that apples fell, but few people were inclined to infer universal principles from these commonplace events.

In emphasizing learning the Institute does not differ from many other centres. For learning has been given an important part in many systems of psychology and a central place in some. The Institute is unique only in the comprehensiveness it attributes to the process and in the consistency with which it uses it as a basis on which a practical philosophy is formed.

[17]Sir Richard Livingstone, *On Speaking the Truth.*

With the Institute's interpretation of "learning" certain psychologists might quarrel. Actually it is assumed implicitly rather than expressed explicitly in most of the studies and publications. The clearest description of it is given in *Understanding the Young Child* (B8).

"Learning" is used to describe the fact that the human being, having few instincts, experiments in his activity and selects those forms which bring him satisfaction. By keeping the consequence of a particular activity consistent, satisfaction is invariably attained by the same means. Such activity is therefore selected by the individual, or is said to be "learned." What adults want a child to learn he will therefore learn more readily if the environment is controlled so that the consequences are consistent. This consistency of consequences becomes the technique of a plan of *discipline,* or training. The child learns in this way to *conform.*

While it is true that much satisfaction is attained through repetition of acts the consequences of which are known (conformity), it is also attained in attempting various activities to discover what consequences will be produced. This is what is meant by *creativity,* and to encourage it, it is necessary to allow the child to experiment in his activity unconcerned with what pattern he will select, but at the same time to limit the possible consequences so that they are never so drastic as to overwhelm him. By this he learns not conformity but creativity, a willingness to accept consequences that he can only partially predict. Only through such learning can he become capable of accepting change, and since both his social world and his environmental opportunities constantly change, his learning to create is as important as his learning to conform.

To indicate the comprehensiveness the Institute assigns to the process of learning, the ways by which it interprets certain concepts in terms of this process will be used as illustrations.

For example, certain psychologists have assumed that preschool children are instinctively jealous of a new baby in the home. Jealousy, either in an adult or a child, is difficult to define. The Institute's interpretation is as follows: It is an observable fact that many pre-school children (although the percentage is unknown) show changes in their behaviour of a disturbed or disturbing sort when a baby arrives. This is the result of the fact that a new and rather complicated learning situation is presented to the child. Having lived in the home for three or four years the child has experienced rather consistent consequences to follow his actions. He has, it might be said, learned his role. With the baby's arrival the consequences he has learned to expect are suddenly changed. (For example, his running to greet his father, which has invariably been followed by a hug, is now followed by his father's hurried effort to see the baby.) If many consequences have changed greatly or drastically the child's learned patterns are upset, and considerable new learning is required. In this learning, emotion arises, reflecting itself in the disturbed action which so surprises the parents. Since the only new factor in the situation is the baby, it is simple for a psychologist to diagnose this as the cause of the disturbance. Whether the pre-schooler himself is equally as good a logician is questionable. Possibly, what he experiences is a feeling of dissatisfaction in his learning and it may be because the adult suggests it to him that he projects this on the baby. From this interpretation, instead of trying to stamp out, or talk out, jealousy in the child, the Institute's programme would be based on searching for ways and means by which the difficulty of this new learning situation could be reduced. How many previously learned consequences can be maintained? How can the inevitable new consequences be introduced gradually and satisfactorily?

Expanded, this approach forms a new outlook for the whole area of clinical psychology and personality problems and therapy becomes a matter of planning particular ways and means by which the disturbed child or adult is enabled to *learn* more satisfactory and satisfying patterns of activity.

A second illustration of the use of the concept of learning may be taken from the area of social living. The need for good social development is given wide expression in modern education and mental hygiene. The Institute would subscribe whole-heartedly to the belief that the modern world requires a high degree of social understanding and participation by all individuals, and that individuals need the experiences of living as social beings. However, it believes that the attainment of these good things, like those of the rest of life, is the result of a long and complicated learning process and occurs neither as the result of instinct nor through the influence of the oedipus or any other complex of early emotional attachment. The child becames social as he learns that the consequences of social activity are satisfying, and in no other way. If his parents plan so that he is able to gain satisfaction through his activity with them, good parent-child relationships will develop. The essence of mother love and father love may remain always a mystery; the expression of it is manifest in the parents' continual acceptance of the child as a learning individual. The Institute believes that the parent-child relation is extremely important in the child's social development, but since he has to live with his contemporaries through his life rather than with his elders, his early learning in his peer group may be equally influential. The complexity of social intercourse for the pre-school child is great. He has neither the verbal nor the cultural skills most social situations require. His natural activity left uncontrolled will probably produce consequences most unsatisfactory to him. He receives hits where he anticipated a hug. Therefore he may, as in any other learning situation, become emotional and withdraw or behave chaotically. From these situations social habits and attitudes develop that subsequently effect his social relations and engender adverse personality qualities. Because of this the Institute policy is to reduce the complexity of early social living to a form simple enough for the child's ability.

Social opportunities and activities are designed, therefore, not to be miniature replicas of adult living but to be formed so that the child can learn the satisfactions of social interaction in ways which he can manage and understand. So in the nursery school and the home social activities, in play, routine, and parties, projects are simplified to meet the child's abilities and supervision is constant to forestall situations arising which would lead to drastic consequences, thereby thwarting the child's social efforts.

Any social world implies social requirements. Where two or three are gathered together there must inevitably be some compromise. The young child has to learn that if he is to enjoy social privileges he must accept social restrictions and requirements. Some centres hesitate to establish any requirements, fearing that by so doing they may set up insidious repressions. The Institute does not believe that by learning to accept restrictions the child need necessarily be repressed. Indeed it assumes that certain restrictions are not nearly as harmful to the personality as the chaos created by complete self-expression. Of course, the child must learn to be creative in his social life but creativity is socially possible in the child or adult only within a framework of conformity—a conformity which at the most mature level is only to the principle of the human good in a world society, at the preschool level to the reasonable requirements which are established for the welfare of living in the microcosm of the nursery school.

Learning "social readiness" pervades the whole curriculum of the nursery school. Social learning is slow, for the content to be mastered is difficult and the skills required are many. Here, more than in any other area, we must not expect too much too soon. Eyestrain from too early efforts to read can be corrected by glasses. Personality strain from early pressures in social living is rarely corrected but only compensated for in the warped social practices so prevalent in our present world.

In our society social education has too often been based on a laissez faire attitude developed through indifference to, or ignorance of the principles of social learning. Because of this attitude, education swings from rigid regimentation that represses the child to free expression, by which it implies that the child should be left to do exactly as he wishes; this latter taken to its logical conclusion would insist that if the child wishes to express the sum of $2 + 2$ as 5, let him. This we would feel may indicate his creative ability but hardly prepares him for his future enterprises in a world which accepts the convention that 2 and 2 equal 4. So too, to let him express himself by "fighting it out," fails to consider the fact that the child on whom he is fighting it out may have his desired form of self-expression severely curtailed, and that this is a misguided form of learning for living in a world which must live at peace if it is to live at all.

The results of our past ignorance of social learning have resulted in the social chaos of our present day. It is true, of course, there is some attempt to offset our ignorance by sporadic efforts in social education. Our schools fiddle with a few courses on citizenship while the world burns. Our children are trained in democracy through learning to adapt the paraphernalia of parliamentary procedure to the function of committees preparing the school dance. We have assumed that by some magic, sports and games develop the essential skills for social living, forgetting that our increasingly terrible Waterloos not only have been won on the playing fields of the past, but may also have been there created. Our hope is that the playgrounds of the nursery will give us a glimpse of what social living can be and demonstrate that while the art of peaceful co-operation is difficult to learn, it is not impossible.

If the Institute has achieved anything towards human understanding surely it is this—that the human being learns, and that this learning can be directed to the socially Good Life. Its rudiments are acquired in the early years, through the child's learning, if not at the mother's knee at least within her ken, and through his practice of the social arts in the graded opportunities of the nursery school. But a philosophy based on the concept of learning has far wider implications. For learning can become a means with which to reinterpret too the broader social problems. Nothing in human nature makes it impossible to learn to live in the present world, even though the consequences of all action are relatively unpredictable and widely ramified. The only difficulty is that learning takes time, and problems where old formulae have to be reorganized before new ones can be achieved require a great deal of time. Our only anxiety is: Will there be sufficient time for our children, if not ourselves, to learn the new attitudes and develop the new techniques the situation of the present requires?

THE SIGNIFICANCE OF EXPERIENCE. A second recurring theme played with variations through the Institute's literature is that a child is a conscious being whose experience grows from his sensory perceptions. These percepttions arise in early infancy predominantly from the tactile, kinaesthetic, and internal senses and later through the distance receptors. Thus the "phenomenological field" develops from impulses from an internal and external *real*, objective world. The translation of these impulses into psychological meaning is dependent on the organization of the total experience of the individual, but it is also defined by the nature of the perceptual processes themselves and their physiological functioning. Through understanding this point of view some interpretation of the development of child experience is possible and by it "adultomorphising" the child's world is avoided.

There is a good deal of evidence to suggest that the distance receptors do not function adequately until some time after the child is born. His first experience arises, therefore, from the "bodily sensations," and it is through the care of these, food, warmth, movement, that his early social and environmental relationships are established. The child is thus predominantly "sensuous" and only later social. The child is aware of his own internal sensations before he is able to perceive an identity of "mother" but it is through her continued association with so many sensations that gradually the deep place she assumes in his experience develops. The beginning of good social relations is founded therefore in adequate methods of child care.

As internal and kinaesthetic sensations continue throughout life much that is discussed as depth personality and emotion have their origin in these. To aid the initial organization of these the training in routines is stressed. If primary experience is organized adequately it is pleasant, and the individual is able to meet the confused perceptions arising from a complex world against an underlying serene pattern (see A2). The complexities of psychological Security have their origin in the incipient experiences of the infant and these can only be controlled through planning of physiological processes giving rise to early experience.

At nursery school age the immediate tactile, visual, auditory, and kinaesthetic sensations are means by which the child increases his conscious experience. His activity is often motivated by the desire for sensory experience. He hits a doll, which may only to the psychologist, and not to himself, represent his father, because the sensations, kinaesthetic and tactile, resulting from hitting are pleasant. He would also hit a block of wood. To the child perceptual reality provides a wealth of interest. Probably the mystery of adult amnesia for the first few years can be understood if we realize that experience at this level is fundamentally perceptual rather than ideational, and perceptual experience is remembered only in imagery, not in verbal forms. The highly perceptual quality of the child's experience probably also accounts for the phenomena of eidetic imagery.

The implications of sensory experience in understanding human beings are many. Consciousness rather than the subconscious or unconscious is significant. The form in which sensations and perceptions enter consciousness and how these are organized and interpreted, create the "inner world" of the individual. Their integration provides ultimately the personality's *feeling* of Security, and the materials from which his imagination, reasoning, and inventiveness arise.

That the psychological problems of the adult go back to childhood experience no one can doubt. And it must be remembered that childhood experience is predominantly of a sensory-perceptual kind. The inner world of childhood is formed of perceptual reality. Our mental hygiene begins with that fact.

This interpretation also has its revolutionary effects. It implies that a good society must provide ways and means by which satisfying sensations can occur. Lessons on good citizenship are rarely heard by children who are enduring the muscular perceptions resulting from long periods of sitting still. Facing reality is hardly intriguing for an adult if such reality holds little that is pleasant in the way of colour, light, sound, touch, or movement. To a culture which values efficiency above enjoyment, only personalities which are perceptually distorted can adjust. A psychologically oriented world must be based on the dictum "except ye

become as little children," remembering that the little child's
judgment of both truth and reality is based on his actual experience rather than on cultural evaluation. He perceives cool, wet
mud as pleasant to touch and move and perhaps to taste. Only as
the culture interprets this as "dirty" and "bad" is he led to question the validity of his perceptual experience and feel the conflict
between psychological primary evidence and adult culturally
defined values. As a "little child" his interest and delight in the
perceptual realities of living mean that although he may later
have to lie to his parents, as yet there is no need to lie to himself.
The Institute has emphatically reiterated the need for helping the
child to continue to enjoy and to enlarge his perceptual world.
It has suggested that it is only as our culture forces the individual
to replace these primary realities by its myths and shibboleths
that he comes to be no longer a little child and consequently
grows incapable of "entering the kingdom."

In the twenty-five years the Institute has progressed towards
greater human understanding. It has assumed that fundamentally
the human being is to be considered an experiencing and a
learning organism. It has clarified the nature of child experience
and it has demonstrated the width of application that may be
made from the process of learning.

It is no longer possible to organize a home, a school, a church,
an army, an industry, a nation, or a world without taking into
account the nature of the human material of which all of
these are composed. Many misconceptions and fantasies
about human nature prevail. Economic myths, religious myths,
political myths, and "common sense myths," confuse parents,
teachers, political leaders, and scientists in their understanding of what are the fundamentals of human activity.
Into this welter of confusion the Institute's clarion note
seems to be this: Of *techniques* and methods for economic
betterment, religious education, international peace, or community welfare we can say very little; these are the concern of
the expert in each field; but we can state that in so far as these
are all concerned with one common factor, namely, the develop-

ing human being, any planning must be based on the known truths about his nature. These truths as we see them are: The human being is basically an experiencing and a learning individual. He is a conscious being whose psychological satisfactions are learned from the adequacy of his experiences in a real world. Bribes, punishments, or rewards of greater wealth, higher social status, community kudos, are at best *ersatz* securities and become necessary only when satisfying primary experiences are denied. For the child a prize is never necessary if his play itself is satisfying; he never needs to be "best" if he is enjoying the goodness of his activity. He never needs to hoard if his wants are satisfied, nor to be hostile if he is not afraid. Natively he never acts to procure a prize, but to satisfy a need or for the purpose of enjoying the activity itself. All human efforts directed to artificial incentives must therefore have resulted from misguided *learning*. Our generations have been *taught* to be competitive, hostile, apprehensive, and insecure. But none of these characteristics is instinctive, rather they have developed by training in which the primary attributes of human beings have been at best misunderstood, at worst deliberately distorted. This need not continue to be so, for through learning all things are possible. With this knowledge available, it is incumbent upon us and those set in authority over us so to plan for ourselves and for our children that the growth of genuine experience and opportunity for ever increasing learning are possible. Based on such fundamentals of human understanding the Good Life would become no visionary hope projected to a remote future, but an actuality of the immediate exemplified in our homes, our industries, and our parliaments, as it has already been demonstrated in our nursery schools. This then is the Institute's contribution to human understanding.

Towards verification. These psychological truths are not self evident. They have been obtained through inquiry and their verification must be in their pragmatic adequacy. The philosophy of the Institute has been demonstrated in its own Nursery School, in the home, with the Dionne quintuplets, and with mental defectives, and has been found effective. Possibly its best demonstration is through the research programme itself. For surely if the children in the Nursery School are privileged to live in a world which expresses this philosophy, the workers in research should equally be entitled to conduct their activities in a similarly permissive environment.

So it has been; the student has dwelt in a world in which he has had to learn both to meet requirements and to use freedom. The requirements to which he has had to conform are those of scientific method; the freedom lies in the scope he is allowed in which to follow his interests creatively. As he, and his staff, are learning, errors are expected and mistakes are considered to be merely sign-posts to new directions. The Director has never dominated the research although his ideas have permeated it. His function has been chiefly maieutic, and never dictatorial.

Whether a rigidly planned programme of research determined by one authority would have produced better results is unknown. Such an approach at the Institute would have been a violation of its own principles. For learning, creativity, co-operation, and widening of experience are as much the right of the research worker as they are of the child. And the verification of the psychological principles in which the Institute believes will come as it is demonstrated that they can be applied successfully with children, with parents, with research students, and ultimately with ourselves.

That each writer has made his own unique contribution to the growth of the research programme is obvious; that the research programme has contributed to the growth of each writer is equally true. For the process is as important as the product. Most goals are mirages vanishing as they are attained. Attainment is always illusionary; the reality is in the attaining.

The hypothesis of this study has been that during twenty-five years the Institute has progressed towards its goal of adapting scientific method to the study of the child and thereby increasing human understanding. The evidence from the documents and the verification from practical life enable us to conclude by writing Q. E. D.

The Documents

The Documents

ACKNOWLEDGMENT

A GREAT deal of appreciation is due to the many individuals who have served as subjects. Without their co-operation, of course, the researches could never have been made. More than 6,550 subjects, ranging in age from infancy to adulthood, have participated. We hope their contribution has been equalled by the enjoyment they obtained.

Special thanks should be given to the many organizations who have co-operated by providing settings in which the studies have been made. Research always involves extra effort on the part of busy supervisors, teachers, and parents and the value of such effort is not always immediately apparent to them. It is hoped that this book will repay them in some small way if through it they see the study carried out amid their busy activities has formed one strand in the pattern of child study and aided our efforts towards the better understanding of children.

In each abstract the name of the organization in which the study was conducted is given. The only exceptions are when the organization was not identified in the original thesis, or the study is being continued at the present time.

A NOTE ON METHOD

The materials produced by the Institute include unpublished reports and studies and published books, monographs, pamphlets, and both scientific and popular articles. From lists which were available in the office files and information from various members of staff a master copy of all the documents was made.

Selection of materials. To decide which documents were to be included in this book was not simple, for a definition of research is not entirely clear. Every study made some contribution to research and all publications reflected some of the results of scientific effort. However, to limit our investigations, it was decided to omit all pamphlets and popular articles and all studies by students below the M.A. level. We included all researches at or beyond the M.A., all scientific articles, and all monographs and books. Two of the monographs are parent education outlines rather than research and none of the books are strictly scientific treatises. However, because they apply to the practical field principles substantiated by research, they have been included.

Further difficulties in selection of *theses* arise from the fact that the Institute of Child Study is not a graduating department. Students using the area of child development for dissertations for the M.A. or Ph.D. present their theses through the Department of Psychology to meet the requirements of the Department and of the School of Graduate Studies. Since the problem to be investigated is chosen by the student there are certain difficulties in determining exactly what theses are rightly counted as "Child Study." For purposes of this book it was decided to include as child study theses:

1. Those which were based on observations of the children at the Institute or Windy Ridge,[5] or on records obtained about these children.

2. Those studies which were directed to an area of major interest of the Institute, or closely supervised by a staff member.

3. Those studies which were conducted by a person who was concurrently a member of our staff and the major part of whose

[1]Windy Ridge is a private day school for children from 2 to 8 years of age. Dr. Blatz is the Director and it has been closely associated with the Institute.

programme was involved in child study. On the basis of this decision theses written by individuals prior or subsequent to their appointment on the staff were omitted although the content in certain cases was related to the Institute's interests.

Studies which were conducted in settings available because of the advisory, consultant relationship of the Institute to an outside organization were omitted unless they met the requirements outlined by the above criteria.[2]

Within these limits this book contains every document we have located, regardless of the calibre of the study. Our records may err in being incomplete, since especially during the early days no systematic list was kept of exactly what studies were carried out at the Institute. Our errors we believe are those of omission rather than commission.

Accepting these decisions it was found that 76 theses, 3 articles, 17 monographs, and 11 books comprised our data.

Organizing the material. In order to condense the materials for inclusion in this book the unpublished theses were abstracted and the published materials briefly summarized.

THE THESES. A letter was sent to every writer of a thesis describing this project and asking for permission to include an abstract prepared by the writer himself or by the research staff. A few writers submitted their own abstracts; these are followed by the authors' initials. Most assigned the task to the research staff. The theses were divided among members of the staff on the basis of familiarity with or interest in the topics. All the abstracts were made according to prepared outlines and insofar as possible reported the information in the words of the original thesis.

The abstracts were read in the first draft by the two senior members of the research staff, checked against the original theses, and prepared in a form of presentation by which readers unfamiliar with the original theses could clearly understand the method used, the main findings, and the interpretation made by the author at the time. By this we hoped to provide a set of documents which would show the

[2]For example, members of our staff have been associated with the Juvenile Court, certain public schools, and welfare organizations. It has been possible for many university students to carry out their studies in these centres because of these associations.

historical development, not only of content but of method. It is quite evident that methods used twenty years ago in certain studies would not be acceptable today; nevertheless it is through the inadequacies of these earlier studies that more sophisticated approaches have been developed. Each abstract was indexed by the letter T followed by a number in chronological order.

The second draft of each abstract was read by a member of the research staff who was comparatively unfamiliar with the original thesis. Minor amendments were made and the complete set of abstracts given to two members of the editorial committee who had not read them previously; with their suggestions incorporated this is the form in which they are given in this book.

Theses on Security: Seven theses of 1949 and 1950 are given only by title. Abstracts of these have been made and are available in mimeographed form at the Institute's library. It is anticipated that in the near future they will be included in a publication by the Director on the Concept of Security and its scientific study.

PUBLISHED MATERIALS. These were read and summarized by the editors of this section. As these materials are already available in printed form the main emphasis in the summaries was to select the salient points that show the study's derivation from or contribution to the general trend of research. These were indexed under the letters A for Article, B for Book, and M for Monograph, and numbered in chronological order.

Presenting the Material. The abstracts and summaries are presented in strict chronological order and each should be self explanatory. If read through consecutively, these documents should provide the reader with the story of the Institute's research. Editorial comment has been curtailed to a minimum and when given is always indicated under the heading "comment." Such remarks serve mainly to draw the reader's attention to influences and relationships between studies, which are not immediately apparent.

1927

A1. BLATZ, W. E., and BOTT, E. A. "Studies in Mental Hygiene of Children. I—Behavior of Public School Children—A Description of Method." *Ped. Sem. & J. genetic Psych.* 1927, XXXIV, 552-582.

Introduction

The chief problem confronting the scientist studying human behaviour is "how to apply scientific methods to the study of those manifold settings in daily life where difficulties of human adjustment take their rise." Essential to this is the development of the right relationship between the scientist and the community organization in which he is studying.

Three points of principle are given:

1. "The investigator's horizon should not be limited to the pathology of behaviour; he must of course studiously relinquish preconceived ideas concerning what is normal and what not, trying rather first to record the salient facts and trends of behaviour under known environmental conditions and with due allowance for the psychological make-up of the individuals concerned." He must study cases from those who offer no concern as well as to the more dramatic problem cases. "This necessitates contact with children . . . in schools as well as in courts, in homes that are successful as well as those where anomalies of behaviour have gotten out of hand."

2. "Longitudinal case study is of paramount importance in mental hygiene . . . one must learn what to record and how. . . . Methods must be adapted to needs and one should feel free to utilize whatever plan of inquiry seems best to suit the problem in hand."

3. "In relating university personnel to public institutions for purposes of research it is helpful to select problems which offer a ground of common interest from the practical as well as the scientific side." The investigator must familiarize himself with the practices of the organization (school) in which he is to work; but he must not assume routine responsibilities in it. "He must learn to participate in a practical situation without making himself indispensable to it."

The Behaviour of Public School Children

The primary interest of this report is its description of the procedures by which a public school was chosen and sufficient rapport developed between the teaching and research staffs to investigate children's problems co-operatively. Through mutual participation the teachers and investigators developed a list of children's *misdemeanours* by which each child was appraised. Continuous records were devised for each child over a four-year period; reports on the methods of handling and classroom summary sheets were organized. The human and scientific factors involved in organizing a recording system in a school form the main interest of this paper today.

An analysis of the misdemeanours of 1437 pupils for the year 1925-1926 are given and lead to the following summary:

1. This study presents an attempt to enumerate and later evaluate in an objective manner the behaviour of children in a particular social environment, i.e., the public school. The study is organized in parallel with other allied researches which furnish additional knowledge of the situation.

2. The detail of the technique employed for behaviour study is elaborated with copies of forms and records. Special attention is called to the manner of classifying misdemeanours.

3. The frequency of the types of misdemeanours, as classified, is given for the eight grades in the school. The number falls off markedly in the higher grades but at different rates for the various misdemeanours.

4. The number of misdemeanours reported is greater for boys than for girls.

5. The frequency is not closely related to chronological age, the greatest number appearing between ages 7 and 9.

6. The frequency of misdemeanours varies inversely with the Intelligence Quotient for boys but not for girls.

7. The data for succeeding years will be analysed along similar lines in order to present a fuller and more accurate picture of the facts than is possible in this initial stage of the project.

1928

T1. PARKER, JANET. *A Comparative Study of Legitimate and Illegitimate Wards.* 1928. Pp. 38.

Problem. To compare legitimate and illegitimate wards of the Children's Aid Society on certain characteristics.

Subjects. 43 illegitimate and 45 legitimate wards of the Children's Aid Society ranging in age from 1 year to 16 years. These children were matched according to age, period of commitment, and on basis of referral to the society, namely "inability of parents to provide suitable homes."

Method. From personal examination by the author, records of the society, from foster parents and relatives, the following data were available: complete physical examination, mental test, social history; present social adjustment; educational status; social adjustment in school.

Results. Summary of data concerning the parental and social background

	Legitimate	Illegitimate
Age of parents:		Greater proportion in the second decade of life
Health of parents:	Mothers in poorer health; greater frequency of venereal disease	
Mental status of Parents:	Greater frequency of mental deficiency and psychoses	Greater number normal and above
Occupational status:	At home	Mostly factory workers and domestics
Social background:	Parents and near relatives show higher frequency of immorality, court record, and alcoholism	

Summary of data concerning children

	Legitimate	Illegitimate
Present placement:		Slightly superior
Physical:		
Height & weight—	Equal	Equal
Structural defects—		Superior
Disease history—		Superior
Intellectual capacity:	16% above 100 I.Q.	Superior, 40% above 100 I.Q.
School standing:		Slightly superior
Conduct:	Equal	Equal

Conclusions. On the whole illegitimate wards of the C.A.S. are a better risk for adoption than legitimate wards from the point of view of heredity, physical and mental equipment, and social background.

In the historical review the author indicates that there is a suggestion from vital statistics gathered from various sources that illegitimate adults are more prone towards social maladjustment than are legitimate. If this be true, it may be concluded from the data in this study that whatever influences are brought to bear on children towards delinquency affect the children after adolescence rather than before. Perhaps the knowledge of their irregular parenthood has an adverse effect during this period, especially if they first hear about it then.

M1. Bott, E. A., Blatz, W. E., Chant, Nellie, and Bott, Helen. "Observation and Training of Fundamental Habits in Young Children." *Genetic Psych. Mon.*, 1928, IV, 1, 161.

Point of View

1. "Each of the studies is undertaken not as a problem" requiring solution, but rather as a systematic exploration of some particular sphere of activity of young children . . . the situation should be without special "controls" (in the sense accepted in most laboratory experimentation), else the findings will not reflect either the customary practice or the complexity of influences regularly at work.

2. The difficulties of observing the varied activities of children, recording the data, and safeguarding accuracy and reliability are noted. These studies suggest a particular empirical procedure. "Two essentials in collecting and cataloguing information will be to deal with points that are unambiguously recordable and if possible quantitatively measurable."

3. The objective in analyzing these routine situations is to formulate from the observed facts some norms of behaviour against which deviations can be evaluated.

The Studies

The observations were based on children at the Nursery School during 1926-1927 supplemented by reports from parents in parent education groups. The methods by which they were recorded have formed the basis of the School's routine records and the results have provided preliminary, factual data on normal development in these areas. From these studies desirable practices and techniques for guiding children's development and methods for treating specific cases began to emerge.

The studies consist of "Sleeping Habits of Children," "Play Activities in a Nursery School" (this included studies of play materials, social contacts, and span of attention); "Eating Habits in a Nursery School"; "Development and Training of Control of the Bladder"; "The Attendance Record 1926-27."

From these studies a plan for supervision and training of the child in each area is given. The emphasis is on the child's ability to learn provided suitable conditions (later called "plan of discipline") are provided. In so far as the stress laid on routines has frequently been interpreted by the public and by other psychologists as a plea for adherence to rigid training schedules, it is interesting to note that the authors make the following statements regarding bladder training— but which are equally adaptable to other habits: *(a)* do not over-emphasize early acquisition or over-train at any stage; *(b)* avoid all disturbing emotional complications; *(c)* employ a training to assist at intrinsic points rather than one based on extraneous motivation; *(d)* aim to develop that rhythm of control which will best be adapted to both the physiological and social needs of the *particular* child.

1929

T2. LANGSTAFF, CARROLL. A Comparison of the Behaviour of Human Subjects and Chimpanzees in Similar Controlled Situations. 1929. Pp. 65.

Problem. To duplicate Koehler's experiments with chimpanzees by using children as subjects in order (1) to compare the behaviour of the two species and (2) to examine the doctrine of insight.

The study is preceded by careful analyses of Koehler's experiments and of his statements regarding learning by insight in apes.

Subjects. Nineteen boys and 11 girls from 2 to 5 years at the Institute's Nursery School, of whom 16 were available for the whole investigation.

Apparatus. Duplication of Koehler's apparatus in so far as it could be adapted for children—(1) various uses of a stick to obtain objective in a cage; (2) making an implement (double stick) to obtain objective; (3) blocks to climb to reach hanging objective. The objective was in a cage 31 inches square, 18 inches high, open on one side, set on a table; the children were outside. The bars were 1½ inches apart and numbered to facilitate recording.

Method. First Series of Experiments

The child was brought individually to the room and simply instructed to get the biscuit or banana. The experimenter recorded his activity on a prepared form.

1A. Two metal rods 23 inches long on table ledge on open side of cage; objective inside.

1B. If after five trials in situation 1A the subject failed to use rods they were placed diagonally through bars touching each other 3 inches in front of objective.

1A (Imitation). If situation 1B were not solved the subject observed a child who had solved 1A repeat his solution. He was immediately brought back to situation 1A.

1C. Two short rods which had to be fitted together to reach the object were placed side by side on the table.

1C (Imitation). The child observed a child who could do 1C and attempted it again.

1D. An obstruction was placed so that the object had to be pushed around it to be attained.

1E. The rods were in the far corner of the room behind the child.

1F. No rods, but an umbrella stood behind the cage.

Second Series of Experiments

The objective was hung in middle of room; the height could be varied with that of the child. Two boxes (A) 16 × 16 × 6 inches and (B) 12 × 8 × 8 inches, when piled to give a height of 18 inches, could be mounted and the object reached. The incentives for both series were "animal biscuits" and later bananas. Each child was taken individually to the test room and told he could have the biscuit (or banana) if he could get it.

The experimenter *recorded* behaviour and vocalization on a prepared form marked in minute intervals. Symbols were used for activities and verbatim reports for vocalization. An outline of differences in Koehler's procedures and the author's is given.

Results. The results are divided into two main sections, (1) the analysis of the children's activity, and (2) a comparison of this with Koehler's reports of the chimpanzees.

1. The children's results are considered as *(a) types of solution:* immediate, sudden and gradual; *(b) types of response:* pertinent, exploration, random exploration, contemplation, abstraction (emotional, giving up), vocalization. Case descriptions of each of these are given in the text; tables of numerical results being based on so small a number of cases, are given in detail in the appendix. There are low correlations, all under $+.25$ between time of solving and M.A. or C.A. However the majority of failures occur with youngest children.

2. The results from the children are compared with those from the chimpanzees in detail on each experiment.

Conclusions. 1. The behaviour of apes and children was similar except for language. The use of a stick as a tool presented equal difficulty to both species. The children were more successful in solving problems which involved building with boxes and removing obstacles. 2. The solutions were of three types: immediate, gradual, and sudden. 3. Four types of response were distinguished—exploration (pertinent or random), contemplation, abstraction, vocalization. 4. There is no evidence in these results of any new type of response significant enough to require a new concept of insight.

Comment. The significant feature of this study lies in the detailed descriptions of each child's process in solving the problem. While the processes may be classified as immediate, gradual, or sudden, the variation among the procedures shown by each child indicates that given a problem, a variety of activity may be used successfully by the subject to solve it. Thus the process of learning will be manifest in many forms.

This material was presented in a paper by Dr. Blatz under the same title and published in abstract in *Proc. Am. Psychol. A.*, 511, 1928.

T3. LESLIE, BAILEY S. A Social Analysis of Juvenile Delinquents. 1929. Pp. 22.

Problem. To evaluate social, educational, and intellectual data of juvenile delinquents.

Subjects. Three hundred and forty-three cases referred to the Toronto Juvenile Court Clinic for one year, October 1926 to October 1927.

Method. Examination of each child included: *(a)* physical examination; *(b)* intelligence test, *(c)* school report, *(d)* report from supervisor of detention home; attitude to authority, etc., *(e)* social history, *(f)* psychiatric diagnosis—including developmental history, *(g)* social agency contacts, (h) staff conference diagnosis—and consensus on disposal, (i) follow-up reports—after 6 months and after 12 months.

Results. The more significant findings were: median I.Q. 85; range 23–144; 61 per cent lived in an intact home—father and mother both living; 20 per cent left school before the age of 16; 62 per cent were making satisfactory progress in school; 77 per cent were reported as socially adjusted in school; 19 per cent were reported as accepting responsibility in the home with reference to home chores, etc.; 50 per cent of the companions mentioned by the children have also appeared in juvenile court; very few have pets or hobbies for leisure time activities; high frequency of bad temper, eating problem, lying, pilfering, enuresis, truancy, and running away (reported by parents).

Conclusion. The author suggests that more important than I.Q., intactness of home, or school progress, is the training within the home with reference to routine discipline especially in the early years.

T4. MALTBY, LILA. The Foster Child of Pre-School Age. 1929. Pp. 56.

Problem. To devise a plan for testing the intelligence and studying the difficulties in social relationships and habit training of children in foster homes.

Introduction. A general description of the Infants' Home is given and an account of the establishment of a mental hygiene clinic in 1927 under the direction of Dr. Blatz. This is followed by an extensive history of child placement.

Subjects. One hundred and ten children (68 boys, 42 girls) of pre-school age in foster homes—under supervision of the Infants' Home Society of Toronto; 86 were of illegitimate birth.

Method. 1. Each child was given a Kuhlmann test with a parent present. Records were kept of child's reaction to test situation and the parent's reactions to the child's efforts. 2. Re-examination after 6–12 months' placement in the foster home. 3. A social history of the home was provided by the social worker. 4. When problems arose the child was brought in by the foster mother for consultation.

Results. 1. From the 50 cases seen during the first year of the study a consultation history based on the categories suggested in *Parents and the Pre-School Child,* was evolved. This included a face sheet and sections on (1) family history; (2) chronology and placements; (3) developmental history; (4) present status of the child; (5) psychological tests and recommendations; (6) progress report.

2. From information collected on these consultation forms analysis was made of certain items: *(a)* The average I.Q. 90, range 46 to 125. *(b)* The difficulties arising in testing infants with suggested methods for meeting them. *(c)* The difficulties reported by foster parents; these included eating, eliminative, sleeping, and play difficulties, emotional disturbances, self-assertive tendencies (disobedience), self-negative tendencies (tics, lying), sex problems. Corporal punishment occurred in 86 per cent of the cases but only in 24 per cent was it severe. *(d)* No correlation was found between the number of problems and number of placements. (A discussion of the statistical findings together with workers' opinions regarding the undesirability of too many placements is given.) *(e)* The relationships of types of problems to age is given. Elimination difficulties decrease from 12 to 23 months of age. Play, sleeping, self-assertion, and eating difficulties occur to greatest extent at 2 years; masturbation at 3 years. Corporal punishment was used most frequently with younger children. Emotional difficulties show a sharp peak at 2½ to 3 years.

Conclusions. The author suggests desirable developments in the work of the Infants' Home with foster children would include (1) parent education; (2) training of social workers in mental hygiene of childhood; (3) opportunities to follow up cases; (4) improved clinical techniques; (5) the establishment of a nursery school.

B1. BLATZ, WILLIAM E. and BOTT, HELEN. *Parents and the Pre-School Child.* New York: Morrow, 1929. Pp. xii + 340.

This, the first book of the Institute, is divided into three parts: The first comprising topics which we have found to be fundamental for parents in the understanding and guidance, of the pre-school child. The second part is a brief exposition of the broader implications of child study and parent education showing their relation to the more inclusive conception of mental hygiene. This is designed primarily for professional workers, graduate students, leaders in parent education and others of like technical interest. The third part consists of forms used in our clinical consultation service and of records for the use of parents in observing their children. (p. iv)

The point of view expressed is:

The emphasis in the field of child study, and especially in connection with behaviour problems of childhood, has generally been placed upon the clinical study of cases presenting peculiar and pathological conditions. Because of this approach we have such concepts as pathological lying, the constitutional psychopath, kleptomania, etc. In this book the emphasis is to be upon a philosophy of training for the "normal" child. (p. iii)

The writer of the Foreword, Dr. Gruenberg, states:

The first-hand studies upon which this book rests are informed throughout with a wholesome appreciation of what it means to keep the growing child in health, especially in mental health. It is a commonplace that knowledge derived from a study of the sick, the disordered and defective should yield guidance in preventing sickness and disorders. In harmony with more advanced thinking, the authors of this book have conceived hygiene in positive terms: it is not sufficient to prevent trouble, it is necessary to insure, through constructive efforts, the optimum development of powers and of satisfaction. (p. xi)

The authors define their approach to the study of children by the following three criteria:

The given datum for study must be the *individual in the ordinary situations of everyday life.* Details of method must therefore be weighed in the light of whether they are readily applicable for the study of fundamental processes and activities discoverable of the individual at home, at school, at work, etc., rather than only in the atmosphere of the conventional laboratory situation.

Secondly, we have sought to view the *individual as a developing person,* hence our concepts must be capable of taking account of progressive changes in the process of growth and adjustment, whether the changes be normal in type or widely divergent.

Thirdly, whatever method is applicable to one level of the growth series, for instance, to childhood, should be capable of *extension without serious recasting* to accommodate whatever increasing complexity of data might come to light in any later phase of the life-series. (p. 283)

They relate the functions of research and education in the following manner:

It will be evident from these postulates, as well as from what has gone before, that our dominating interest in the field of child study is *investigation* and that we conceive the educational functions of group or individual contacts to be subsidiary to this primary purpose of finding out more facts about the child. This is as much a principle of pedagogy on behalf of investigators who are being trained as it is a direct object of an institution existing for purposes of research. The interrelations of teaching and research as they exist in our Universities need defining, and in no field is this more pertinent than the one of child study. It is our experience that active participation in a situation is the best incentive to its study; and conversely, that research justifies itself when its results and methods are utilized as the basis of a teaching program. Therefore, in emphasizing investigation as the essential in a program of child study, research should not be thought of as an isolated interest, but always in relation to the practical outcome. Moreover, in referring to effective teaching as a practical outcome of child research, more is implied than the technical training of selected students as skilled personnel. We mean in addition that the research outlook should be so conceived and carried on that its results and practice will be applicable in meeting that broader educational need now felt by parents, teachers, social workers and others who have constantly to deal at first hand with children. The interests of mental hygiene will always, and legitimately, scrutinize the fruits of research in child psychology to see wherein the results assist in the interpretation and management of concrete human situations so that accurate individual diagnosis and constructive preventive measures may be thereby facilitated. (p. 284-285)[3]

The content for parent education is limited primarily to habit formation and the emotions, topics on which research had already been carried out (M1) or was in progress (T9, T10). The authors state that other aspects of child training are being reserved for a later book (B2). Habits are considered as learned forms of behaviour that are of value both as means of saving time and energy and as fundamental patterns for social life. Yet they emphasize the "plasticity of the organism and the possibility, even in mature life, of developing new habits and modifying old ones. In short, the learning process is co-extensive with life." (p. 36)

Comment. This emphasis on learning is basic throughout later researches and becomes the crux of the Institute's philosophy of development.

1930

T5. DAVIS, M. A. An Evaluation of the Criteria for Selecting a Good Foster Home. 1930. Pp. 41.

Problem. To make a quantitative analysis of the principal criteria currently used in the selection of foster homes for children. To determine to what degree each criterion is operative.

Materials. The records on 218 homes applying for children for foster care, follow-up records on approved homes, and refusal notes on those rejected.

Method. Quantitative analysis of the data on these records.

Results. 1. Forty of the 218 applications were approved for foster homes.

2. The differences between "approved applications" and "total applications" were found on such factors as age of parents, nationality, occupations, weekly income, home ownership, number of rooms, number of children, health, religion, experience with children, etc.

3. Since none of these differences is significant, it is concluded that they are not absolute standards, but relative to each other and must be weighed in every case by the worker's judgments. However, it is pointed out that items about any home which deviate too far from

[3] Reprinted by permission of William Morrow and Company, Inc., New York.

the median of the data for the group are to be used as negative criteria in selecting that particular home.

T6.   Gordon, Gretta H. The Adjustment of Two-Year-Old Children into the Nursery School Situation. 1930. Pp. 43.

Problem. To devise a method of studying the adjustment of children to a nursery school setting that would provide data allowing for quantitative analysis. Adjustment is considered as progress in adapting to a social environment.

Subjects. Three children entering the Institute's School, January 1930.

Setting. At this time eighteen children attended. A regular daily programme was laid down from 9.30 o'clock including routine and play periods. On the child's first day at school he remained until 11 o'clock and the mother stayed with him.

Method. Records were kept on the three children during the full school day for the first twenty days of attendance. For the first five days the experimenter kept a detailed running commentary. On the basis of these records a systematic system of observation was set up as follows—the child's behaviour was noted in nine separate routine situations to which he must respond daily. Categories were: co-operative, unco-operative; slow. (Records of play periods were not used in the study.)

Results. Data obtained on the three children are presented qualitatively and quantitatively. Individual differences are shown in the degree of adjustment, the rate of adjustment, and in the situation to which adjustment is made.

Conclusion. It is concluded that behaviour adjustment to nursery school situations can be recorded systematically and objectively so as to yield results indicative of individual differences. It is suggested that the relative value of the different situations for measuring adjustment requires investigation.

Comment. This was an introductory attempt to devise daily records for initial adjustment to nursery school.

T7.   Johnson, Frances Lily. A Genetic Study of Distraction in Young Children. 1930. Pp. 48.

Problem. "To study the relationship which the distraction time of pre-school children bears to the time spent in occupation with materials where the occupation has a work aspect and the materials are used in a prescribed manner." By distraction is meant a break in attentive adjustment. A detailed review of the philosophical and experimental studies of distraction is given.

Subjects. Twenty-one children at the Institute of Child Study, ranging in age from 2 to 5 years, 7 girls and 14 boys, with a median I.Q. of 125.

Material. Work bench and real tools, which children were taught to use in the prescribed manner. Defined tasks were given in order, so that a child had to complete one task before he could proceed to the next.

Method. Each child was observed in the school workshop for five periods of 30 minutes each, at weekly intervals, with three other children present. The observer tabulated any interruptions from the task and their length by a stop watch. At the end of the period of observation the type of interruption, the total time spent in work and the total time spent in distraction as well as the number of distracting episodes was calculated.

Results. 1. It was found that the types of distraction could be classified into eight categories; the frequency of each type falls into the following order: watching (occupying 45 per cent of total distraction time), talking, playing with materials, idling, interfering, imitating, co-operating, and playing with child, 38 per cent of total distraction time.

2. There are no apparent sex differences in types of distraction except in the more infrequent distracting episodes—imitating, co-operating, and play with child.

3. There is a correlation of −.57 between age and amount of time spent in distraction.

Conclusions. There is a decrease in distractibility with age.

This study illustrates the complexity of any situation with reference to the interests of individuals. Any aspect of the environment may be considered a distraction provided an arbitrary set is initially determined. It is possible to classify, record, and measure various influences which affect continued effort in any one direction. Certain common trends have been indicated by the method employed although there are individual differences as in all aspects of behaviour. (F. L. J.)

T8. LEWIS, RUTH. A Study in Training Children of Very Low Mentality in Eliminative Control. 1930. Pp. 57.

Problem. This study was arranged to test whether the plan of training used for normal children in toilet training was applicable to institutionalized children of the idiot and imbecile classification.

Subjects. Twelve boys in Ontario Hospital, Orillia—C.A. 5–14 years; M.A. 1 year 2 months to 3 years 10 months; average I.Q. 23 (Kuhlman). All children had enuresis.

Setting. All 12 boys were housed in infirmary room. Separate playground with suitable play equipment provided. Two nurses were assigned to their care.

Method. The whole day was planned to meet the needs of the children. Nursery school routine was arranged. Play time, sleeping time, eating routine were all arranged according to a schedule. Regular prescription for toilet training was begun. If necessary each child was taken to toilet every two hours during day time. Gradually as the child acquired control the interval was increased. A chart of eliminative function was kept for each child as well as a chart on play activities both outdoors and inside.

Results. All children responded to the treatment. Seven cases were cured and remained so after one year. In the worst case daytime but not night control was established. Six of the cases were transferred to the lower school and were making good progress. There seemed to be closer relation of C.A. than M.A. with rapidity of training. The children who participated most in the play activities showed a more rapid rate of learning control.

Conclusion. 1. Methods of training in eliminative control successful with normal children are applicable to children of low mentality. 2. Children of higher C.A. responded more quickly than younger children irrespective of M.A. 3. A consistent routine in other areas, viz., eating, sleeping, play times, etc., was conducive to successful training.

T9. RINGLAND, MABEL C. A Study of Tics of Pre-School Children. 1930. Pp. 56.

Summary of Method. In order to make a quantitative study of tics in pre-school children, twenty-five Nursery School children were observed on two occasions each (16 of these at more than one age level), and also 46 public school children in Kindergarten and Grade 1. All observations were taken individually, over a half-hour period, except in Grade 1, where they were taken for fifteen minutes. A careful record was kept of all tics occurring during these periods. It was found that they could be classified in thirteen different categories.

Conclusions. 1. Tics are an extremely common form of reaction in pre-school and first-grade school children. 2. The mouth is the most frequently used part of the organism in tics. 3. Between the ages of

2 and 7 the frequency of tics increases with age. 4. Tics are about equally frequent in girls and boys. 5. Tics occur with greater frequency when gross bodily movements are inhibited, either by reason of occupational restraint or the restraint of sitting at tables and desks. 6. Certain phases of school life tend to foster the development of superfluous and undesirable movements, which in extreme forms are regarded as serious abnormalities. (Published 1935; see M4.)

T10. STARR, ALIDA. Emotional Episodes in Nursery School Children. 1930. Pp. 32.

Problem. To study the emotional behaviour of pre-school children as it occurs in the nursery school situation. To analyze the situations which give rise to the emotional behaviour.

Subjects. Two groups of children 2 to 5 years of age attending the Institute Nursery School. Group A—18 children; Group B—16 children.

Setting. Observations were made throughout the day, 9 a.m. to 3 p.m., upon all the children in attendance. Group A was observed over a five-month period; Group B over a three-month period.

Method. Records were kept by the staff in charge. Each incident of emotional behaviour for every child was recorded separately by all adults witnessing it, on forms provided. Emotional behaviour was objectively defined as disturbing behaviour. Records included—time of day; apparent cause, behaviour, treatment, duration.

Results. 1. Frequency of emotional episodes decreases with age both individually and as shown in cross-sectional comparison. Frequency in adult supervised situations decreases as age increases. 2. The immediate situations in which the emotion arose were classified into 14 categories. Relative frequency of these varied with age and length of time of attendance. The older children showed increased frequency in emotional situations involving other children and staff discipline. 3. Behaviour during emotion was classified under ten headings. All forms of behaviour occur throughout the age groups; crying occurs with the same relative frequency throughout. Hitting and sulking occur more frequently with the older group. The older children · tend to show more complex behaviour patterns, involving attempts to adjust to the situation. No specific relationships could be found between type of situation and behaviour used.

Conclusion. Emotional behaviour is subject to genetic changes in terms of frequency; and situations giving rise to emotion and behaviour response. Two-year-olds express emotion in a stage of resistance to adult supervision. Under a consistent routine this decreases and is replaced by an acceptance of conventions.

Comment. This was a preliminary attempt to record emotion in children and to devise forms by which such episodes could be incorporated into the regular records.

B2.   BLATZ, WILLIAM E. and BOTT, HELEN. *The Management of Young Children.* New York: Morrow, 1930. Pp. xii + 354.

The second book of the Institute is written for leaders in parent education and focuses on the problem of socializing the child, a subject about which "the authors admit there is little evidence by way of scientific studies."

> For the social emphasis of this book we make no apology. The most important task which children have to learn is to live with others on a basis of mutual satisfaction. We have endeavoured to outline what we consider the underlying principles of the child-parent relationship rather than to present detailed results of experimental work or systematized observations with children. This is largely because of the dearth of scientific studies with children, particularly of studies designed to bear directly upon the issues that parents actually encounter. Child Study is still a young science, and while its easier and more obvious aspects have been fairly well charted the more complicated questions of social relations, the development of personality, etc., are only beginning to be approached in any thoroughgoing fashion. Meanwhile parents are living in the midst of situations which can ill afford to wait till authoritative pronouncements are available for their solution. Can something useful be done in the meantime from such data as are at hand?" (p. v)[4]

Following a consideration of the ways in which a parent may best help a child to become social the authors state "*we have assumed throughout that learning is the most significant of all functions in the developing child.*" (p. vii) They consider the development not only of good parent-child but indeed all other social relationships as the result of a learning process.

1931

T11.   FLEMING, MAE. A Method of Evaluating the Home Discipline of the Preschool Child. 1931. Pp. 36.

Problem. To discover measurable factors by which home discipline may be evaluated as an aid to *(a)* clinical diagnosis, *(b)* evaluation of foster homes.

[4]Reprinted by permission of William Morrow and Company, Inc., New York.

Subjects. Twenty-nine children in attendance at Nursery School at Institute of Child Study, 17 boys and 12 girls, ranging in age from 2 years to 5 years.

Setting. Homes of the children.

Method. Each Nursery School child was observed in his home for a period of four hours from 10 a.m. to 2 p.m.—records were kept of the child's behaviour in the various activities in the home, i.e. playing, eating, sleeping, etc. A satisfactory and unsatisfactory adjustment to each situation was worked out in conjunction with staff of the Institute, e.g. in Play: Satisfactory—keeps himself happily employed, uses material constructively; Unsatisfactory—disinterested, long periods of aimless activity. A *score* was calculated in terms of a percentage of possible "satisfactory" items observed.

Results. 1. In the homes studied the score (average) of the activities was Play—96; Sleeping—91; Eating—88; Washing—82; Elimination —81. The author attributes the high scores to the fact that not only were the homes in the upper socio-economic bracket but the parents had all attended parent education classes over a period of 2–5 years. 2. The most frequent "unsatisfactory" item recorded was "failure to allow child to assume responsibility."

Comment. The record for home visits prior to school entrance was based on this study.

1932

T12.   MACNAMARA, J. G. A Preliminary Analysis of the Results of the Rorschach Test. 1932. Pp. 17.

Problem. To determine the responses to the Rorschach test of a group of children differing in age, and to compare these with the responses from a group of normal adults.

Subjects. One hundred and ninety in all. Children from a nursery school, a kindergarten, and from Grades 1, 2, 3, and 4. Age range from 30 months to 179 months. (The schools are not identified in the thesis.)

Materials. The Rorschach test.

Method. The test was administered according to Rorschach's directions; then the protocols were scored according to his categories of location, determinants, and content.

Results. 1. Age variations were found in number of responses. The number increased from an average of 12.4 with the nursery school children to 35.3 for Grade 4. However for "details" the oldest and youngest children gave fewer replies than the middle groups. 2. Indications of age difference in form and colour appear. Pure colour responses occur in 17 per cent of all the answers and in 27 per cent of those of the youngest group. Instead of colour-shock most children expressed enjoyment of the colour cards. Colour-form answers drop from 70.6 per cent in the youngest group to 17 per cent in the oldest. Form-colour answers vary from 10 per cent in the youngest group to 83 per cent in the oldest. 3. In content it was found 48 per cent of all first answers were "animals." This was fairly constant through the age groups. In decreasing frequency for the whole group were found answers of landscape, lifeless objects, natural phenomena, pure colour, humans, and geography. Age variations occurred in all these. 4. Comparing children's answers with Rorschach's on adults it is found (*a*) none of the age groups fits exactly into his normal or abnormal group; (*b*) the nursery school results are similar to "manic" normals; (*c*) Grade 3 results are similar to "orderly schizophrenics"; (*d*) Grade 4 results are similar to average normals.

Conclusions. Rorschach's conclusions on adults are not directly applicable with normal children; one must establish norms for each age level. By so doing the development of ideation in children could be studied.

T13. MILLICHAMP, DOROTHY A. The Development of Emotion in the Infant. 1932. Pp. 44.

Five children were observed for three consecutive days of each month from the first month to two years of age. The records were kept by the parents, trained under supervision of the Institute of Child Study.

The emotional episodes were assembled from the complete records and analyzed.

The analysis of data showed:

1. Emotional Frequency—a consistent decrease with age, with periodical fluctuations similar in the five subjects.

2. Emotional Behaviour—a genetic sequence of behaviour types showing an increase in complexity and adjustive quality with increasing age. These behaviour types are similar to the behaviour activity appearing in non-emotional situations.

3. Emotional Situations—a possible separation of emotional situations into three main divisions: (a) Thwarting of Non-Specific Approach Attitudes; (b) Thwarting of Specific Approach Attitudes; (c) Thwarting of Specific Withdrawal Attitudes. Each division showed a peculiar frequency distribution common to the five cases.

4. Conclusions—the emotional life of an organism starts when the experienced situation cannot be adequately dealt with by means of the response repertoire available at the time. Differentiation occurs through the innate mechanism of approach and withdrawal, the basis for the development of the attitudes. There appear, early, two gross forms of emotional behaviour which may be termed anger and fear, positive and negative, or x and y. The complicated emotional experience of later life is due to the growing complexity of total situations depending, not on change in this fundamental character of emotional experience but rather upon whether the conflict pertains to sex, hunger, rest, self-assertion. (D.A.M.) (Published 1935; see M5.)

T14. McFarland, Elda. An Analysis of the Paintings of Preschool Children. 1932. Pp. 42.

Problem. An investigation of spontaneous creative activity in preschool children (painting). This was considered from the following points: (1) colour; (2) subject matter; (3) design; (4) self-criticism; (5) stages in development.

Subjects. Twelve four-year-old children, 10 three-year-old children, 8 two-year-old children.

Apparatus. Easels, paper 12 × 18 inches, 10-inch paint brushes, four primary colours placed on chair.

Method. In all, 848 paintings were examined. A total of 158 paintings was observed and recorded upon during process; records showed (1) colours chosen; (2) subject matter; (3) development and design; (4) conversation and remarks.

Conclusions. 1. (a) There are no colour preferences. (b) Colour is used (1) as a medium for expression; (2) for appreciation and stimulation; (3) to represent the elements of an object or situation. (c) Colour is not used representatively with its true value.

2. (a) The younger child does not spontaneously name his paintings. (b) The older child's description of his subject matter falls in two types (1) single word; (2) composition.

3. (a) There is a design form produced by first strokes of brush. (b) Design is present in four forms: rhythm, repetition, balance, and

symmetry. *(c)* Design is deliberately attempted by four-year-old children. *(d)* Individual characteristics are recognizable. *(e)* Design is not a separate stage in Development (as Cottrell implied in her study).

4. Self-criticism is a development at the four-year-old level.

5. *(a)* There are three types of conversation, assignable to three age levels. *(b)* There are two stages in development (1) manipulative, (2) representative. *(c)* Imitation is not an influencing factor. *(d)* Children of pre-school age do not paint from a model. (E. McF. B.)

T15. STAPLEFORD, ELSIE M. A Study on Resistance in Pre-School Children. 1932. Pp. 32.

Problem. To study the nature of resistance, and to note its occurrence among pre-school children in *(a)* the relatively uncontrolled nursery school environment, and *(b)* the controlled mental test situation. To relate resistance to "perseveration" as measured in a controlled setting. By resistance is meant a child's tendency to oppose requests made of him or to refuse to comply with what was expected of him. Other studies have called this behaviour "negativism."

Subjects. Thirty subjects, 14 boys and 16 girls, ranging in age from 27 to 59 months.

Method. 1. A measure of perseveration was obtained following Cushing's procedure—e.g. length of time a child continued to play with two given toys was measured.

2. Data on resistance were gathered over two terms *(a)* by staff observations recorded on prepared forms of occurring instances; *(b)* analysis of routine records; *(c)* analysis of playground records; *(d)* incidents occurring during the administration of a Kuhlmann test. A total of 1219 instances of resistant behaviour were collected.

Results. 1. *Perseveration* time ranged from 2 to 38 minutes. It showed some relationship to age. On a re-test the reliability was −27.

2. *Data about resistance show:* *(a)* Amount of resistance in the nursery school shown in the routine records: of 5060 occasions on entrance and nurse's examination in which resistance might have been shown only 29 incidents occurred. In toilet routine: 30; in food reports: 327. In play an average of 2.3 cases of resistance per child were found. *(b)* Resistance could be classed under nine headings according to the type of situation arousing it. These were routine, discipline, suggestion, offer of help, rules, leaving parent, food, mental test, and other children. *(c)* There is a decline of resistance with age in every class except that of resistance to other

children. *(d)* I.Q. and resistance to adults show an inverse relationship. There is no relationship between I.Q. and resistance to other children. *(e)* Seven correlations between amount of resistance in different situations were obtained. These were all low, −.12 to +.16 and as the P.E.'s are large it is impossible to say if there is any significance.

Conclusions. Incidents of resistance can be observed and obtained from records although they are few in the nursery school. They decrease with age and I.Q., indicating their disappearance with growth of co-operation. The low inter-correlations suggest a specificity of resistance rather than it being a generalized trait. (E. M. S.)

Comment. The outstanding finding of this study is the very small number of "resistances" shown by children in a situation which is based on knowledge of the child's abilities and in which direction is given and help offered only when the child needs it.

1933

T16. FRED, BEATRICE V. A Study of Companionship among Pre-
school Children. 1933. Pp. 21.

Problem. To investigate factors operating in the selection of companions by nursery school children.

Subjects. Sixteen boys and 14 girls between 2 and 5 years of age at the Nursery School, Institute of Child Study.

Apparatus. Record sheet for each child to show with whom he was in contact during each of 24 five-minute observations.

Method. Observations were made on the playground of each child to discover with whom he was playing during the period. These were analysed to show length of contact, companions of older and younger age levels, of the same and opposite sex.

Results. 1. Most contacts are of short duration. 2. Four-year-olds and two-year-olds play chiefly with their age mates; three-year-olds show more spread in their contacts. 3. Participation in larger groups increases with age.

Comment. This is the first of the theses to consider social behaviour. The writer has difficulty in devising a method by which social contacts may be accurately observed and analysed. This difficulty was being clarified by Bott's investigations (Child Development monographs 1 & 2).

T17.   GAGE, BEATRICE. A Method for Investigating the Moral Judgment of Young Children. 1933. Pp. 28.

Problem. To devise a method for the investigation of moral judgment in young children. A chart showing investigations of moral
judgment from 1896–1932 is given.

Subjects. Twenty-three children from the Institute of Child Study,
2-4.11 years; 40 children from Windy Ridge 3.7-10.6 years.

Apparatus. A puppet show placed on a low table in front of the
child (stage about 2 feet long with all the equipment, curtain drops,
and scenery similar to a real theatre stage). Experimenter sat behind
the table, hidden from view by screens, and manipulated 4-inch high
puppets which were attached to pieces of leaded wire. Grooves in the
stage floor allowed the experimenter to manipulate the puppets from
beneath the stage.

Method. Presentation of three short "plays" involving "unjust"
punishment for the child. At the end of each play 15 questions were
asked. Some of these required mere understanding of the plays, others
involved "moral" judgment.

Results were based on the children's answers to these questions.
Responses were classified as follows:

1. *Adequate* (a direct and pertinent answer to the question).
There were very few adequate responses from children under 3;
between 3 and 4 years, not quite 50 per cent of the responses were
adequate; between 4 and 5 years by far the majority of children were
giving adequate responses; and after 5 years there are very few cases
of inadequate responses.

2. *Interpretation* (an adequate response containing some explana-
tion or reason). Although older children gave a much higher percentage of these than younger children, it was felt that the questions
had not been worded in such a way as to make this classification
satisfactory.

3. *Responses Showing a Knowledge of Consequences* (i.e. indicating a moral judgment). All children over 3 who answered the
questions adequately appreciated the mechanism of consequence, e.g.
stated what should happen next. There was a definite increase in the
frequency of expression of consequence with chronological age but
not necessarily a knowledge of its true nature.

Conclusion. A fairly high percentage of "adequate" responses was
obtained from children under 6 years old, which leads to the belief

that by making certain improvements discussed in the text, this method could be used with success in further investigation. Discussion of the judgments obtained shows that the expression of "moral" judgment tends to increase with the subject's age and that the principles applied in these judgments were specific rather than general. (B. G.)

Comment. This study, which was an attempt to bring the more general earlier approaches (e.g. Piaget) to an experimental form, was further developed in the later investigations of Long (T40) and McKay (T50).

T18. GRIFFIN, JOHN D. M. A Guide for the Taking of Psychiatric Histories and the Examination of Children. 1933. Pp. 57.

Problem. To construct an outline guide for clinical history-taking and examination of children, with the purposes of providing a systematic method of reporting case material (1) to increase understanding of the patient, and (2) to provide a form in which data would be available for research.

Materials. Current standard authoritative sources on history-taking methods; the author's clinical experience.

Method. A longitudinal approach was taken, covering all the pertinent physical and mental aspects of the individual's development. An outline of headings was prepared, with the kind of material to be elicited under these headings described and defined, both for the history-taking up to the time of onset of illness (anamnesis), and for the psychiatric and physical examination of the child.

Results. 1. An anamnesis and an interview outline that serve the dual purpose of enabling complete coverage of psychiatric material as well as providing organized material for research. 2. A rationale for these outlines that stresses the importance of the understanding of the individual as a dynamic, developing entity. 3. The functions of the psychologist as psychometrician, objective appraiser, and member of the interviewing team are outlined. 4. Examples of complete histories and interviews are provided.

Conclusion. The author's contributions (aside from providing a teaching aid for psychiatric personnel) are: (1) his insistence on a developmental approach, whereby the individual is studied in relation to his own behaviour "norms"; (2) his stress on appraisal in terms of the dynamics of development, rather than by a cross-sectional description such as was obtained by psychiatric classification alone;

(3) his suggestion that cross-sectional analysis be used in studies for prediction; (4) his emphasis on research. (See also entry M7.)

T19. HUSBAND, MARGARET L. The Food Preferences of Nursery School Children. 1933. Pp. 28.

Problem. To study the eating habits of a group of Pre-School children as a basis for evaluation and revision of methods of training.

Subjects. Twenty-nine children in attendance at the Institute Nursery School ranging in age from 2 through 4 years.

Setting. Observations were made at the noon-day meal at the Nursery School for 120 days covering a six-month period. The meal was a regular dinner dietetically planned. The children ate in age groups of two to four children with one adult. The regular dining-room procedure was followed.

Method. Daily recordings were made of eating behaviour by the staff in charge. These included order of eating, amount eaten, and refusals of food. A total of 2476 observations was obtained.

Results. Order of eating food and refusals were found unreliable as criteria for measuring food preferences. Using frequency of second servings as the best index of preference the following results appeared: Stewed foods are most preferred; creamed are least. Preference appeared for foods having definite form; for meat, fish, and eggs as compared to vegetables; for bland foods. Preference at the three age levels showed the same tendencies with some increasing preference for foods having form and distinctive taste with age increase.

Food refusals occurred in 1.4 per cent of total possibilities and decreased with age.

Conclusion. It is suggested that with further study to verify results, children's indicated preferences might be used to plan their menus so that foods available were acceptable. Eating habits might thereby be improved. "To what extent should we allow children's preferences to govern our selection of menus and to what extent should we try to govern the child's preference?"

T20. SMITH, ALATHENA J. The Development of a Mental Hygiene Programme under Public School Auspices in a Small Suburban Community. 1933. Pp. 43.

Problem. A report on the demonstration of a general mental hygiene service in the school system of Shorewood, Wisconsin (population 14,000) 1930-1932.

Subjects. School children registered in Public Schools, 1300; High Schools, 1230.

Method. 1. In this community provision was made for: *(a)* In service training of teachers in mental hygiene. *(b)* Tax-supported parent education. *(c)* Early contact with pre-school children. *(d)* Specially trained personnel to carry on this programme.

2. New services incorporated under this scheme: *(a)* A home visit to each child of 4 years who was not already enrolled in order (1) to discover why he was not enrolled; (2) to urge parents to take advantage of pre-school education for the child. *(b)* Arrangement for special classes or tutors for retarded children, hard of hearing, crippled, with vision defects, deaf, with speech defects, with serious personality deviations. *(c)* Individual case work—children referred by administrative officers, teachers, and parents. Number of children referred (1930-1931), boys 55, girls 27; (1931-1932), boys 85, girls 42. *(d)* "Summer Round Up" of children who would enter school for first time in the fall. Physical and mental check-up.

Results. After the two-year demonstration these services were permanently incorporated into the school system. A suggested child guidance clinic was not founded, however.

A2. BLATZ, WILLIAM E. "The Physiological Appetites," in *Handbook of Child Psychology,* second edition, edited by Carl Murchison. Worcester, Mass.: Clark University Press, 1933. Pp. 723-770.

This is the first systematic statement of the physiological appetites which are given a fundamental place in Blatz psychology. In place of instinct theories, the author describes six physiological processes which are modified through learning to meet cultural requirements. He describes the physiological background, rhythm, conscious aspect, innate response, modifications and maladjustments of the appetites of hunger, thirst, elimination, rest, change, and sex. From an understanding of these emerge plans for child training and the development of the routines.

M2. BOTT, HELEN McM. *Method in Social Studies of Young Children.* Child Development Series, No. 1. Toronto: University of Toronto Press, 1933. Pp. 110.

The shift in method of studying personality from the use of rating scales, diaries, and verbal responses to direct observation has been caused by a desire for greater objectivity and an exact portrayal of social behaviour. This monograph is a detailed description of how such observations may be made, recorded, analysed, interpreted, and expressed. It reports the difficulties in the objective approach and indicates how these may be reduced.

The list of categories under which social behaviour is to be observed is outlined and compared with those used by other investigators. Methods of measuring reliability are described by the author and a chapter on the use of statistical methods is given by S. N. F. Chant.

This outline has been used in many of the studies made at the Institute and has provided the basic method for investigating social behaviour.

1934

T21. BARTLETT, ROSE. An Analysis of the Daily Home Activities of Preschool Children. 1934. Pp. 26.

Problem. To investigate the possibility of study of young children's activity in their homes by using parent observations. The assumption is made that the home programme of activities and the child's adjustment to these is a significant aspect of his experience. There is an extensive review of early literature and research dealing with this point.

Subjects. Twelve parents attending a parent education group at the Institute. Thirteen children of the above parents, ranging in age from 2 to 5 years.

Materials. Two record forms were devised. Form A: 31 activity items were enumerated. Parent was required to fill in time each activity was begun. Form B: Twenty possible responses for each activity were listed. Parent was required to check which of these occurred.

Method. Investigation was discussed at a meeting of the parent group. Parents volunteered participation. Records were kept by parents for seven consecutive days. An interview followed.

Results. 1. Investigation of Method: Parents showed co-operation; interest and effort and ability to follow instructions. More precise forms are required. 2. Investigation of Activities: Programmes for the 13 subjects were markedly regular for each and similar to each other. Play varies most. Percentage time spent in each activity was calculated and compared with recommended schedules. 3. Investigation of Responses: The incidence of various types of responses in the different situations was calculated. Voiced objections, 54 per cent; dawdling during meals, 50 per cent; unfavourable responses in play, 28 per cent.

Conclusion. The results of this study indicate that it is possible to obtain data on children's behaviour through parent observation. From the analysis of data it is suggested that if norms of home activity and child response were set up, a technique similar to the above could be used for surveying a particular home and advising parents regarding difficulties.

T22. BLUMENTHAL, S. An Analysis of the Learning Capacity of Young Children to Reproduce Notes. 1934. Pp. 22.

Problem. To investigate the musical potentialities of children through an examination of their ability to identify and reproduce various notes. To see if environmental influence is a contributing factor in the acquisition of this.

Subjects. Twenty-five children ranging in age from 4 years to 9 years from the Institute and Windy Ridge Day School.

Apparatus. Two xylophones, each one an octavo in range, from middle C to upper C. One xylophone was placed in front of the child, while the other, behind a screen, was used by the experimenter.

Method. The child's ability to reproduce on his xylophone the same note played by the experimenter was measured. An *achievement* score for this capacity was obtained by recording all the trials required to complete the series of tasks twice without error. Each child was tested for a 10-minute period three times a week for 10 weeks. Eleven tasks in all were designed.

Information as to the child's musical experience was obtained through a questionnaire and a score for musical experience assigned. The children's Intelligence Quotients, Chronological Ages, and Mental Ages were computed. Musical Achievement as measured here was then examined in relation to these factors.

Results. 1. The errors, time, and trials were recorded on a prepared record form. Thus three scores were obtained; these added together formed a "total score." The correlations between the sub-scores ranged from $+.90$ to $+.97$. 2. The musical achievement scores are arranged by quartiles and the quartile ranking of the child in each other variable compared with these. 3. The results indicate musical achievement to be related to C.A. and M.A.; but not to I.Q. or musical experience.

Conclusions. A method for measuring musical achievement in the child has been outlined. From this the indication is that musical achievement is closely related to general development as reflected in M.A. and C.A. and very slightly, if at all, to musical experience and I.Q.

T23. DALE-HARRIS, MARY. A Study of the Form and Content of Earliest Memories. 1934. Pp. 24 + iv.

Problem. To study the form and content of earliest memories.

Subjects. One hundred and forty-nine students at University 19—49 years of age, average 25 years. 58 girls—8 to 14 years, average 11 years.

Method. The students were given a week to write an account of the earliest experience they remembered. This was submitted with their sex, age, age at time of the experience, evidence of corroboration.

The girls wrote their account at school and took home the paper for parents' signature as a check of authenticity.

Results. 1. *Age of earliest memories.* Girls 36 months, range 16 months to 87 months. Women average 43 months, range 21 to 75 months. Men average 47 months, range 27 to 99 months. 2. *Number of facts.* Average 11.47, range 2 to 53. 3. *Sense modalities.* Ninety-eight per cent had definite sensory background. 4. *Analysis of sense modalities.* Visual 74 per cent, kinaesthetic 57, auditory 45, touch 11, equilibrium 7, pain 5, taste 5, temperature 4, olfactory 1, organic 1. 5. *Affective tone.* This was mentioned in only one-third of the accounts; 14 per cent pleasant, 23 per cent unpleasant. 6. *Emotion.* Thirty-nine accounts mention fear and five anger. 7. *Location.* Seventy-eight per cent familiar settings; 24 per cent unfamiliar. 8. *Social.* Eighty-three per cent people present, absence 15 per cent, adults 87 per cent, children 31 per cent. 9. *Comparison of children's and adults' memories.* Children's "memories" are earlier, include fewer facts, describe fewer sense modalities, kinaesthetic predominate over visual, have fewer mentions of feelings, more references to strange places, mention children less frequently, have higher proportion of pleasant memories.

Conclusions. Early memories have a definite sensory background and a mild affective tone. The physical and social environment are strongly marked; the individual's earliest memory is likely to be of an event which is an ordinary part of his everyday life. Memory content changes with experience; this is indicated by the differences in reports of men and women and children in this study.

T24. POTTLE, HERBERT L. An Analysis of Children's Lies with Particular Reference to a School Situation. 1934. Pp. 30.

This is an analysis of the lies reported between 1926 and 1932 in the "Misdemeanour study" of public school children. (See A1.) It is one of the completed sub-units of the community studies now in progress. (See p. 72.)

T25. WILLIAMS, A. L. A Study of Religious Attitudes in a Group of Adolescent Boys. 1934.

M3. BOTT, HELEN McM. *Personality Development in Young Children.* Child Development Series, No. 2. Toronto: University of Toronto Press, 1934. Pp. 139.

The method of social study described in the author's previous monograph (M2) is applied to 28 nursery school children over a period of seven weeks, during their outdoor play.

The results are considered under measures of social and material activities, verbal and motor activities, relations among children, relations with adults, personal activities, and use of materials.

The results show that positively correlated with C.A. are play with two or more children, conversation, social motor behaviour, social verbal categories, total verbalization, constructive activity, and use of constructive materials.

Negatively correlated with C.A. are playing alone, watching, aimless activity, use of manipulative materials.

Uniform throughout the group were play with one child, routine use of material, total motor activity, use of gymnastic and locomotor toys.

Traits peculiar to individuals were relations with adults, talking to self, tics, and laughter.

The author in appraising the study emphasizes the fact that personality includes the organization of the individual's inner life of appetite and emotion, attitude, desire, and thought as well as action. These studies of his contacts with the outer environment through use of materials and social relationships offer only a partial analysis of his personality, which is justified at the present because such activities are amenable to objective observation. These observations of external adjustment produce a scale of social maturity against which a child's progression may be measured and serve as a basis from which an inquiry into the inner organization, *"integration,"* of the individual, may be made.

The writer thus introduces a point of view which permeates the series of studies, namely, that objective observations of behaviour do not give a complete picture of the psychological individual. Nevertheless it is necessary to clarify overt action before one can seek inner significance.

Comment. As the author states, all aspects of the individual from his appetites to his social relationships play a part in effecting the balance (integrity) of the personality. In reviewing the studies of the Institute it is apparent that many years have been devoted primarily to defining the myriad forms of observable activity. Observable activities having been clarified, the search for the inner integrating principle has become re-defined in the recent studies of the concept of Security. (See M15.)

1935

T26. BOWERS, NORAH K. The Effect of (*a*) a Low Protein Diet and (*b*) an Iron Deficient Diet on Learning in the Rat. 1935. Pp. 37.

Problem. To determine the effect on maze learning ability of a low protein diet and an iron deficient diet.

Subjects. 106 albino rats divided into four groups—a protein deficiency group, an iron deficiency group and two control groups.

Apparatus. Water maze with 16 culs-de-sac.

Method. Learning and retention scores were obtained and the deficiency groups compared with the control groups.

Results. There were consistently better learning scores for control groups over the deficient groups, but differences are not statistically reliable.

T27. BROWN, HELEN C. An Analysis of the Technique for Training Pre-School Children in Eating Habits in the St. George's School for Child Study. 1935. Pp. 32.

Problem. To study the development of eating habits of children in a nursery school setting and to evaluate adult methods of directing the child's behaviour.

Subjects. 27 pre-school children attending the Institute's Nursery School 1933-1935. Age range, 2 to 5 years.

Method. Eating habits are defined to include attitude towards food as well as response.

A systematic observation of each child was made daily by the staff in charge during the regular noon day meal.

A total of 3762 noon-day records were thus obtained. Maximum number for one child was 130.

Every incident of behaviour requiring adult treatment was recorded together with the type of adult treatment used and the result. Defined categories were used and recording was done by symbol.

Results. 1. Behaviour interfering with eating was divided into nine types and 1569 incidents of such behaviour were recorded, e.g. one to approximately two meals. 2. There was a general decrease in frequence with age. All the categories followed this trend except social play and conversation which increased as an impeding form of behaviour. 3. Dawdling remained most frequent throughout the age levels. 4. Adult direction was divided into 18 types. Decrease with age is shown in physical assistance and routine direction, increase in social redirection, and removal of child. 5. During an experimental week when adult interference was cut to a minimum unfinished meals increased markedly in the two-year-old group. 6. During the regular experimental period 110 unfinished servings were recorded in the 3762 meal records.

Conclusion. Behaviour that impedes eating is largely the same as behaviour impeding other routine learning. There are relatively few food difficulties per se, and these occur largely at the two-year level and are therefore reduced through learning.

Any training programme for eating must concern itself with general as well as specific development. Such a plan is suggested on the basis of the data—involving the physical environment, type, preparation, and serving of food, procedures and adult guidance including assistance and direct and indirect control but omitting coaxing, bribing, ordering, or forcing.

T28. MARGOLIS, EVA. A Comparison Between the Achievement of Pupils in a Progressive School and That of a Similar Group of Pupils in a Public School. 1935. Pp. 28.

Problem. To compare the achievement of pupils in a progressive school with that of a similar group in a public school. The comparison was made (i) on the basis of time given to various school subjects; (ii) achievement measured by objective tests related to C.A., M.A., and grade placement.

Subjects. Twenty-five children in Grades 2, 3, and 4 at the Hillcrest Progressive School (H.P.S.); a matched group of 25 children from Earlscourt Public School (T.P.S.); the matching included C.A., M.A., I.Q., school grade, sex, percentage of school attendance in previous year.

Apparatus. The New Stanford Achievement Test involving paragraph meaning, word meaning, spelling, language usage, literature, arithmetic reasoning, arithmetic computation.

Method. The tests were administered at the same time in each school and scored according to standardized directions. The actual amount of time spent on each subject since the pupils had entered school was computed.

Results. 1. There were no significant differences between the groups on any variable. 2. When the subjects are divided into grades, C.A. groups, M.A. groups, and the achievement of these groups compared there are no significant differences. 3. Correlations between M.A. and achievement are .91 (T.P.S.) and .88 (H.P.S.). 4. The H.P.S. pupils spend about 20 days a year less at school than the T.P.S. Just over half as much time has been spent at the H.P.S. on "tool" subjects.

Conclusions. 1. No significant difference in achievement in the two schools was found. 2. But the H.P.S. attain this achievement in about half the teaching time of that of the T.P.S. Thus the methods used in the progressive school do not seem to hinder the child's achievement of basic school skills and content.

T29. MASON, MOLLY. A Study of the Influence of Instruction on the Learning of Pre-School and Elementary School Children. 1935. Pp. 18.

Problem. To discover whether the types of instruction (positive, negative, minimum) used in teaching children varied in their influence with increasing age.

Subjects. Forty-two children ranging in age from 2 years 11 months to 9 years 6 months. These were divided into three groups, I, II, III, matched for C.A. and M.A. Only right-handed children were selected.

Apparatus. Mirror-drawing situation. Cards were mimeographed, a picture of a cat, and, at 8 to 16 cms. distance, a picture of a dish of food.

Method. Mirror drawing was used; the child was asked to draw a line from the figure of a cat to a figure of food. The task was made more difficult by *(a)* separating the "cat" and "food" to a further distance, and *(b)* by placing a barrier of a line on the paper between cat and food which the child in tracing a path had to circumvent without touching it with his pencil. Group I—positive instruction, e.g. "move your pencil this way." Group II—negative instruction, e.g. "don't move your pencil that way." Group III—minimal instruction— the children were told only to keep the pencil on the paper and avoid the obstacles in question and then left to their own resources. Each child was scored on *(a)* number of trials for completion of the task; *(b)* actual time elapsing during trials; *(c)* number of errors.

Conclusions. The main contribution of the study lies in the adaptation of this type of problem (mirror drawing) for use with children. Tentative conclusions from the results obtained from the small number of subjects in each group are:

Positive instruction is most effective at pre-school age level, but *minimal* instruction is most effective at the older age level. Perhaps with the older group verbal instruction is ignored and hence serves as a distraction once the meaning of the task is understood.

T30.   ORD, NAN. Play Interests of the Pre-School Child. 1935. Pp. 19.

Problem. To trace development in play behaviour and interests in terms of *(a)* active use of material; *(b)* frequency and duration of use of material.

Subjects. Twenty-seven children at the Institute Nursery School ranging in age from 2 through 4 years.

Setting. 1. Junior and senior playrooms of the Nursery School during the regular play periods. 2. Experimental playroom equipped with six new materials, one of each type used in the play rooms.

Method. Each child was observed for 14 fifteen-minute periods during the Nursery School play period over 4 months and for 2 fifteen-minute periods alone in the experimental setting.

Recording: Play activity was categorized as *(a)* using material actively; *(b)* not using material actively; *(c)* social activity without material. The material used was recorded. Four children were observed simultaneously. In setting *(a)* one judgment was made at minute intervals; in setting *(b)* at 5-second intervals.

Results. 1. Children use materials actively 50 per cent of time. 2. Time spent in active use of materials increased from second to third to fourth years. 3. Length of time using one material increased from second to third and fourth years. 4. Number of materials actively used per period decreased from second to third and fourth years. 5. Number of different materials used during total time of observation decreased from second to third and fourth years. 6. Preferences, measured in terms of frequency and duration of use, were as follows: 2 years—pattern materials; 3 years—skilled and constructive materials; 4 years—skilled materials. Preferences were more outstanding at the three- and four-year level. 7. Analysis of data in the two settings showed similar trends.

Conclusions. Results indicate a development between two and five years in terms of greater control, organization, and direction of the child's active use of his environment. This is described as indicative of growth in the habit of "interest." The author discusses a concept of interest based on developing control of the act of attending in satisfaction of the "need for change." The developmental process as reflected in the data is outlined as a continuum in which constructive activity gives rise to more skill which gives rise to more selective and prolonged attention or increasing interest which in turn results in greater effort, further increase of knowledge and skill, increasing attention, and more decisive interest. (N.O.F.)

T31. WALKER, ELSIE M. H. Trends in Companionships of Public School Children. 1935. Pp. 26.

Problem. To study the public school child's choice of playmate as stated by himself.

Subjects. Two hundred and sixty-seven boys and 256 girls from Grades 1 to 8, Regal Road Public School.

Questionnaire. One question asking the names of the subject's friends.

Method. 1. Each child was asked individually to name his friends; after ten seconds' hesitation the question was terminated. 2. Information about each child and each friend he named was entered under headings age, sex, grade, school, address, on a two-way card. 3. Reciprocated choices were noted. 4. I.Q. and M.A. were available for 343 of the subjects.

Results. 1. Correlations between characteristics of the subjects and persons named as friends were: Chronological age $+.73$; Mental age $+.63$; I.Q. $+.16$. 2. The relationship on basis of school grade showed that at each grade level the largest percentage of children named as friends were in the same grade as the subject, but choices were made over a wide range of grades, though a very few were given to children in other schools. 3. Age range. Subjects choose most friends within a year of their own age, but the choices ranged over as much as 12 years, the greatest spread being found in Grades 1 and 2. 4. A very small percentage of choices go to children of the opposite sex. The percentage decreases steadily from about 9 per cent in Grade 1 to 1 per cent in Grade 8. 5. An attempt to work out reciprocated choices was based on calculating the total possible reciprocal choices and taking the actual ones found as a percentage of this. The percentages so obtained for each grade were very small (.2 to 1.4 per cent).

Conclusions. This study suggests that selective factors influence choice of companionship.

Comment. This study is of particular interest because it shows how cumbersome it was to handle data of inter-relationships before the use of sociometric techniques. The author raises many of the problems later studied sociometrically but finds the data unwieldy for statistical analysis. However her study also shows that sociometry, while overcoming many technical difficulties, may have done so by ignoring certain important social relations, i.e. those that go outside the defined group of the classroom, grade, and school. It should warn sociometrists their approach covers only a limited aspect of an individual's total social field.

M4. BLATZ, W. A. and RINGLAND, MABEL CREW. *A Study of Tics in Pre-School Children.* Child Development Series, No. 3. Toronto: University of Toronto Press, 1935. Pp. 58.

See study T9, to which an extended review of the literature and of the theories of tics has been added in this monograph.

M5. BLATZ, W. E. and MILLICHAMP, D. A. *The Development of Emotion in the Infant.* Child Development Series, No. 4. Toronto: University of Toronto Press, 1935. Pp. 44. (See study T13.)

B3. BLATZ, WILLIAM E., MILLICHAMP, DOROTHY and FLETCHER, MARGARET. *Nursery Education: Theory and Practice.* New York: Morrow, 1935. Pp. xv + 365.

For the past ten years the contents of this book, developed through experience of failure and success, have been used in the training of nursery school teachers and in the enriching of parent education programmes. In seminars and staff conferences the various aspects and phases of nursery school procedure have been discussed and evolved. For our own clarification it was decided to collect the results of our labors, not in any spirit of finality or as any permanent crystallization of view-point, but rather as a specific starting point for criticism, evaluation and elaboration. (p. vii.)

We are more emphatic about the positive training in the simple things of the preschool child's life because we feel that perhaps we understand these aspects more fully than the complex social and emotional patterns. These latter are still, in a large measure, sealed volumes. The authors feel that they have been afforded a few peeps therein, or rather a few myopic glances. Further research and study will, no doubt, open the book wide and clear the vision. (p. viii.)[5]

The book is divided into a discussion of the theory underlying nursery school education and a description of the practices used in that setting. These practices emerge from research material much of which is quoted or referred to in the book, thus the *Routines* described are an outcome of studies of children's habits (M1, T15, T27), *work and play habits* include information on play activities and materials (M1, T30), painting (T14), and music (T22). Much of the information in the chapter on *social adjustment* is based on observations of children's social activities (M2, M3) and the section on *emotional adjustment* gives evidence from studies of emotional episodes (T10, T13). Record forms which have been derived from research studies and have been incorporated into general use of the school are reproduced.

Comment. The first two books translated scientific knowledge of children for parents; this demonstrates the influence of such knowledge on nursery school practice. Since it has become a text-book for nursery supervisors and was used as a guide in the establishment of Dominion-Provincial Day Nurseries during the war, it is an example of how far the influence of scientific principles gained through research may reach.

B4. POPPLETON, MARJORIE and BLATZ, WILLILAM E. *We Go to Nursery School.* New York: Morrow, 1935. Photographs by John M. Waterman.

A story book for children with photographs illustrating the day's activities at the Institute's Nursery School.

1936

T32. RABINOWITCH, DOROTHY. The Effects of Success and Failure on Learning. 1936. Pp. 12.

Problem. To study the influence of success and failure on persistence of attack in a specific learning situation. (The author differen-

[5]Reprinted by permission of William Morrow and Company, Inc., New York.

tiates between "error" and "failure"—failure being considered the point at which the subject gives up the task.)

Subjects. Fifty-one public school children in Grades 5 to 7 were divided into three groups equated on basis of sex and range in age and I.Q.

Apparatus. Two types of form boards were devised—the first could be fitted together (solvable) and second could not be fitted (insolvable).

Method. 1. In all groups each child was given as a preliminary task a solvable puzzle and the time taken to complete it recorded. 2. Group 1 was given six successive "insolvable" puzzles. Group 2 was given four successive "solvable" puzzles followed by one insolvable. Group three was given a solvable and insolvable puzzle alternatively for 5 trials. 3. Time that the child persisted at each task to success (completion) or failure (giving up) was recorded in seconds. 4. Persistence scores were designed in which the amount of time spent on the subsequent insolvable tasks was calculated as a percentage of the time spent on the first insolvable task.

Results. 1. Group 1 persistence score: task 3, 51 per cent; task 5, 23 per cent. Group 3 persistence score: task 3, 81 per cent; task 5, 42 per cent. 2. Boys persisted slightly more than girls. 3. There were wide individual differences in scores. 4. General behaviour patterns accompanying failure were many, including tapping, banging, grimacing, sighing, etc. 5. The subjects' manipulation of the materials showed individual differences.

Conclusions. Failure is definitely detrimental to persistence. Continuous failure is more detrimental than failure interspersed with success.

M6. STAFF OF THE ST. GEORGE'S SCHOOL FOR CHILD STUDY PARENT EDUCATION DIVISION. *Outlines for Parent Education Groups, Pre-School Learning.* Child Development Series, No. 5. Toronto: University of Toronto Press, 1936. Pp. 67.

Written especially for parent education group leaders, this shows how plans of child care can be based on research findings and supported by research evidence.

M7. BLATZ, W. E. and GRIFFIN, J. D. M. *An Evaluation of the Case Histories of a Group of Pre-School Children.* Child Development Series, No. 6. Toronto: University of Toronto Press, 1936. Pp. 24.

A clinical examination was given to 60 children referred to the Institute because of difficulties and to 60 children, who were not giving apparent difficulty, in attendance at the Institute's Nursery School. The history form used was devised by Blatz (see B1) and incorporated with modified form by Griffin (see T12).

The following conclusions were drawn:

1. Faulty discipline in the home, inadequate development of self-assertion and self-negation, sleeping difficulties, and faulty bladder training are the commonest points of difference between problem and non-problem children. These categories had the greatest absolute difference in frequency.

2. Thumbsucking, nailbiting, other habit tics, and delayed speech appear to be the least important points of differentiation. These categories had the least absolute difference in frequency.

3. Environmental factors (faulty discipline, inadequate accommodation, etc.) occurred more frequently (absolutely and relatively) in the problem children than in the non-problem children. Similarly the proportion of positive environmental categories to positive symptomatic categories was much higher with problem cases than with non-problem cases.

4. Multiple factor analysis of the tetrachonic correlations of the history categories yielded two major factors. Factor I is prominent in the environmental categories and is especially important in the social inadequacies of the home, faulty discipline, and poor accommodation. It is present also in those symptomatic categories dealing with emotional difficulties and inadequacies of the self-tendencies. Factor II is present in the categories related to training, such as difficulties in play and elimination.

M8. BLATZ, W. E., ALLIN, K. D. and MILLICHAMP, D. A. *A Study of Laughter in the Nursery School Child.* Child Development Series, No. 7. Toronto: University of Toronto Press, 1936. Pp. 31.

This study tabulates the various theories of laughter and the stimuli which have been found experimentally to elicit laughter in children. It then describes situations in which laughter occurred based on observations of some 90 children in nursery schools.

From this the authors conclude "Laughter and probably smiling may be considered as socially acceptable tics or compensatory motor mechanisms accompanying the resolution of conflicts that have, for a shorter or longer period, kept the individual on the horns of a dilemma." Thus they advocate an emotional release theory of laughter.

Comment. This is one of the few studies devoted to expression of "positive" emotional states which have tended to be overlooked both in observational approaches to development and also in later forms of personality appraisal.

1937

T33. CHARLES, MARION. Motion Pictures vs. Direct Observation—a
Study of Method in Social Analysis. 1937. Pp. 27.

Problem. To investigate the use and possibilities of motion pictures
as an observational technique in the study of social behaviour of the
pre-school child.

Subjects. Eight boys and 7 girls from the West End Creche Day
Nursery. Age variation from 1 year 9 months to 3 years 7 months.
These were divided into three age groups of 5 children each; I,
average age 25.6 months; II, 29.4 months; III, 39.6 months.

Apparatus. A prepared record form for entering each social contact. A motion picture camera recording social interaction.

Method. 1. The children were brought in groups of five to the playroom of the Institute. A supervised free play period was arranged
using the Nursery School equipment. The children were accustomed
to this procedure. 2. Each child was observed for ten minutes, recorded
in half-minute intervals on four occasions approximately one month
apart. 3. All social contacts were recorded descriptively according to
the actual overt action observed. 4. To facilitate recording each child
wore a large letter on his back. 5. Two observers recorded and their
agreement was 82 per cent. 6. A separate set of records was made
from the motion pictures. Finally all the observations for one child
were entered on one sheet.

Results. 1. The data on social behaviour were increased by the use
of motion pictures, 72, 67, and 69 per cent in groups I, II, and III.
2. The additional data did not change the picture of social behaviour
for the group as a whole, but did change the picture of the child as
an individual. 3. The motion pictures showed many variations of
behaviour not in the observers' records. 4. As the motion pictures were
repeatedly observed each child's behaviour gradually was identified as
having a definite individual pattern.

Conclusions. 1. The permanency and accuracy of observation by
motion pictures renders this invaluable as an observational technique,
especially in the study of individual differences. 2. Because of the
expense of motion pictures a combination of these plus trained observers appears to be the best method. 3. Motion pictures of outdoor
play would have been less expensive because the supersensitive film
would not have been necessary. (Published 1937. See item M11.)

T34. McFarland, Mary. An Analysis of the Social Contacts of Fifteen Preschool Children. 1937. Pp. 43.

Problem. To study by use of motion picture records (1) age differences in frequency and types of social behaviour; (2) individual patterns of social behaviour and their inter-relationships within each group.

Subjects. Eight boys and 7 girls from the West End Creche Day Nursery. Age variation from 1 year 9 months to 3 years 7 months. These were divided into three age groups of 5 children each; I, average age 25.6 months; II, 29.4 months; III, 39.6 months.

Apparatus. A prepared record form for entering each social contact. A motion picture camera recording social interaction.

Method. 1. The children were brought in groups of five to the playroom of the Institute. A supervised free play period was arranged using the Nursery School equipment. The children were accustomed to this procedure. 2. Each child was observed for ten minutes, recorded in half-minute intervals on four occasions approximately one month apart. 3. All social contacts were recorded descriptively according to the actual overt action observed. 4. To facilitate recording each child wore a large letter on his back. 5. Two observers recorded and their agreement was 82 per cent. 6. A separate set of records was made from the motion pictures. Finally all the observations for one child were entered on one sheet.

Results. 1. Age differences. (*a*) There was no significant relationship between number of social contacts and age. (*b*) When the social contacts were divided into eight types it was found *watching* decreased with age −.17; *physical contact* (hitting, slapping) decreased with age −.38; *approach and withdrawal* (coming beside or moving from a child) decreased with age −.61; *gestures* did not relate to age. *Verbalization* increased with age, .81. *Parallel play* was greatest in Group II; *unco-operative use* of materials (interference) decreased with age −.70. Co-operative use of materials had no relationship with age but was much higher for all three groups in the last observation than in the first one four months earlier.

2. Patterns of social behaviour. (*a*) The contacts each child gave and received were set in graphic form. In contacts given three types appeared: (1) the child who divides his contacts almost equally among the four others in his group (four cases); (2) the child who gives more social contacts to one child than the total of the other three (eight cases); (3) the child who directs many more contacts

to two of the children in the group than to the other two. This analysis indicates the child's form of social preference. It is suggested age differences are related to these forms, Type 3 being found to predominate in the three-year-olds. *(b)* The child was also classified according to types of contact he received. The results from *(a)* and *(b)* indicate a high degree of social selectivity. Reciprocal contacts were also studied.

Conclusions. 1. No significant change is found in quantity of social contacts in this age group (1 year, 9 months to 3 years, 7 months). 2. In qualitative analysis the forms of social behaviour change in this age period. 3. Patterns of social relations vary among the individuals and more selective preferences appear with increased age.

Comment. The author indicates that while using such a small group gives difficulty in reaching definite results, yet it enables detailed records to be made of each child's activity and aspects obscured in more statistical analysis are retained. This study and T33 were conducted on the five children as an attempt to devise a method for studying social behaviour among the Dionnes. (See M12-17.) (Published 1937. See item M11.)

T35.   STIRLING, MARGARET E. An Analysis of the Questions Asked by a Group of Pre-School Children in a Controlled Setting. 1937. Pp. 20.

Problem. To study the quantitative and qualitative variation in questions asked by pre-school children—as related to age, intelligence quotient, and experiential background.

Subjects. Fifty-two children including 21 children 2½ to 3½ years; 18 children 3½ to 4½ years; 13 children 4½ to 5 years. Two groups are represented—Institute Nursery School (privileged)—27 children, average I.Q. 107; two nursery schools for underprivileged children—25 children, average I.Q. 99.

Apparatus. Material used to elicit questions was chosen to be both familiar and unfamiliar and included ten objects varying from a can-opener to live rats; ten pictures. Selection was tested in a preliminary experiment.

Method. Material was presented to each child individually in scrambled order one at a time without comment. Time was controlled. Children's questions were recorded and answered. On the following day the material was against presented and the child was asked a routine set of questions and his own questions were recorded.

Results. 1. With increased age more children ask questions and there was increase both in number of questions per child and in number of situations asked about. 2. A similar trend towards increased frequencies was shown by the privileged group as compared with the non-privileged. 3. With *age increase,* a decrease was shown in questions of "Classification"; an increase in questions of "Purpose and Cause" and of "Time and Place." *Order of frequency* throughout age levels was first Classification, second Purpose and Cause, third Time and Place. 5. The *privileged* group asked relatively less of first type. 6. There were more correct answers to both routine and individual questions with age increase and more correct answers given by the privileged group. 7. A positive relationship is suggested between number of questions asked and correct answers. 8. Questions were more frequent in some situations than others irrespective of age.

Conclusions. It is concluded that as children's questioning is related to age it must bear a relationship to developmental factors. Data suggested a positive relationship with mental development; increased experience, and development of the phenomena of interest.

M9. Bott, Helen McM. *Adult Attitudes to Children's Misdemeanours.* Child Development Series, No. 8. Toronto: University of Toronto Press, 1937. Pp. 21.

1. Twenty-one misdemeanours of children of public school age were studied by the method of paired comparisons and scale values assigned by Thurstone's method of attitude measurement.

2. Teachers, parents, public health nurses, social workers and mental hygienists were measured.

3. Ten traits were ranked of relatively the same importance by all five groups; these, in order of seriousness, being cruelty, deceit, sex misdemeanours, stealing, bullying, sulkiness, tantrums, laziness, quarrelling, teasing.

4. Eleven traits were differently ranked. The teachers and mental hygienists differed most in their estimates. Teachers ranked destructiveness, disobedience, uncleanliness, profanity and impertinence as important; mental hygienists regarded these as relatively unimportant. Mental hygienists regarded avoidance of the group, daydreaming, shyness, lack of application, enuresis and mannerisms as important, whereas teachers regarded these as distinctly less important.

5. Parents, nurses and social workers occupied a middle position between these two extremes, social workers agreeing most closely with mental hygienists.

6. The study points the need of agreement on fundamental issues among those responsible for the child's behaviour.

M10. BLATZ, W. E., CHANT, S. N. F., and SALTER, M. D. *Emotional Episodes in the Child of School Age.* Child Development Series, No. 9. Toronto: University of Toronto Press, 1937. Pp. 45.

A study of the incidence of emotion expressed through the overt behaviour of crying, pushing, hitting, sulking, etc. of children 5 to 16 years in three settings, school, camp, and a hospital for the feeble-minded. Records of the type used at the Nursery School (see T10 and T13) were kept by the staff at the school (see A1) for the school year 1929-1930 and at the camp and hospital during the summer 1936. The results are analysed into "incidence of emotional episodes, emotional behaviour and antecedent situation."

The authors conclude:

In general the findings of this observational study indicate that emotional behaviour varies with regard to both chronological and mental development. The variations are indicated with reference to three features of the behaviour: (a) incidence, (b) form of behaviour and (c) type of situation which evokes emotional behaviour. In all of these the inference is that emotional development being essentially unadaptive is modified by learning, the rate of learning being influenced by intelligence. The modifications are manifested in two ways: (a) by a decrease in the incidence of emotional behaviour as the child learns more adequate forms of adaptation, (b) the emotional behaviour itself, becoming less chaotic and better directed towards the problem situation as well as more socially acceptable. As in all learning chronological maturity and mental maturity are influential factors, the development being dependent upon neither to the exclusion of the other. It would appear advisable therefore that the demands made upon the child should be considered from the standpoint of both his chronological and mental maturity, and the relationship between them as expressed by the I.Q. Pedagogically, the implication in these data would be that emotional training can best be advanced by guiding the child in developing more adequate forms of behaviour, thus reducing the prevalence of un-adaptive behaviour. Punishment or mere discipline with regard to emotional behaviour would appear to occasion even more behaviour of the same kind, but perhaps of a somewhat different type. What is needed is facilita-tion of the learning of adaptive behaviour, intelligent guidance, reasonable routine and demands commensurate with maturity apparently being the way to promote this. In this way the occasion for extreme forms of emotional behaviour becomes reduced and a tendency to attack a problem in a less chaotic manner may be acquired.

M11. BERNHARDT, KARL S., MILLICHAMP, DOROTHY A., CHARLES, MARION W. and McFARLAND, MARY P. *An Analysis of the Social Contacts of Pre-School children with the Aid of Motion Pictures.* Child Development Series, No. 10. Toronto: University of Toronto Press, 1937. Pp. 53. (See items T33 and T34; also M12.)

M12. BLATZ, W. E., CHANT, N., CHARLES, M. W., FLETCHER, M. I., FORD, N. H. C., HARRIS, A. L., MACARTHUR, J. W., MASON, M. and MILLICHAMP, D. A. *Collected Studies on the Dionne Quintuplets.* Child Development Series, Nos. 11 to 16. Toronto: University of Toronto Press, 1937.

This includes a biological study of the Dionne quintuplets, and studies of their mental, social, language, and self-discipline development, also a study of their routine training.

The methods for observation and analysis of behaviour derived by previous investigations are here adapted to the unique group studied. Many aspects of the Dionnes' development are compared with norms established by previous or concurrent investigation of children at the nursery school.

The chief contribution to scientific knowledge is the variation the quintuplets show in behaviour, abilities, and personality in spite of their common heredity.

1938

T36. BAILEY, NORA. An Analysis of Camp Records. 1938. Pp. 46.

Problem. 1. To devise a method by which an individual's progress at a camp may be indicated. 2. To provide a basis for organizing a counsellor's training course.

Introduction. The outline of the theory of child training underlying the camp programme was discussed under the following topics: 1. Development of habits of persistent attack on problems. 2. Development of habits of congenial social behaviour. 3. Acceptance of routine responsibilities.

Subjects. 174 boys, 104 girls at related summer camps.

Materials. Record form (sample given) to check: *(a)* Interest (1) persistence (2) activities. *(b)* Social co-operation. *(c)* Incidence of discipline.

Method. These records were kept for one week by the cabin counsellors.

Results. By analysis of the records it was found: 1. The majority of campers carry out responsibilities in routine and elective activities. The girls are better than the boys. 2. Frequency scales of activities were devised showing marked individual differences among the campers. 3. Records of co-operation showed the type of social contacts for boys, girls, older, and younger children. 4. The records of discipline showed that only 12 problems, serious enough to require help from the personnel director, arose with girls and 6 with boys during the week.

Conclusion. The study shows certain of the difficulties in establishing a recording system for a summer camp. It indicates the values and weaknesses of the system in use and indicates the basis on which revision should be made.

T37.   BENSEN, MARGARET. An Analysis of the Imitative Behaviour of Thirty Pre-School children. 1938. Pp. 35.

Problem. To measure the amount of imitative behaviour in terms of age differences in the pre-school child.

Subjects. Thirty children at the Institute's Nursery School. The children were divided into three age groups of ten each, a two-, a three- and a four-year-old group.

Setting. Observations were made on the children in three experimental settings varying in type of play materials used. 1. Raw materials of clay and plasticine on two different tables, two chairs at each table. 2. Paper equipment, blocks, form boards, and manipulative toys on two tables. 3. Large building blocks, doll's furnishings, and small mechanical toys placed around the room.

Method. Each child was observed for 9 fifteen-minute periods, three times with a child his own age, three times with a child 18 months older or younger than he, and three times with two other children, differing from him in age by one or two years. In all there was a total of 270 observations. In each grouping the child was observed in the three settings. Observations were made over a period of four months.

Recording. Each act of "imitation" and of "watching" was timed and recorded descriptively. Imitation was always preceded by watching. "Delayed imitation" was noted.

Results. 1. Types of material showed no difference in their effect on the amount of imitation. 2. The duration and frequency of imitation is greater at the three-year level than at the two- or four-year level. 3. A child tends to imitate either an older child or a contemporary in preference to a child younger than himself. 4. Imitation tends to decrease when the size of the group increases from two to three children. 5. There is an interrelationship between imitation and watching behaviour. Watching decreases as age decreases. 6. Imitation was divided into 3 categories—imitation of (a) a specific act, (b) general movement, (c) vocalization.

Conclusion. From these data imitation appears as an inevitable form of behaviour in pre-school children. Age is indicated as one factor affecting imitation, further investigation should reveal others. Such study contributes in a small measure to the understanding of suggestibility and more widely of social interaction.

T38.   BROWN, ISABEL. An Exploratory Study of Teasing. 1938. Pp. 28.

Problem. To study teasing by investigating the following factors— subject matter; response to being teased; age and sex differences; relationship of teaser.

Subjects. One hundred and fifty university students, 120 women and 30 men, ranging in age from 19 to 24 years.

Method. A questionnaire was presented requesting a record of all incidents of teasing the subject could recall from early childhood up to the present, under the following headings—age and school period; content; by whom; response as resentment or acceptance; past and present attitude.

Results. 1. 1203 incidents were reported. Data suggest an increasing frequency up to high school followed by a decrease which is more evident for girls than boys. Subject matter was categorized as follows: (a) Characteristics referring to self, (1) appearance, (2) behaviour— (i) emotions, (ii) skill,, (iii) habits, (iv) attitudes. (b) Characteristics referring to others, (a) family, (b) outsiders.

2. Frequencies indicate that one is more likely to be teased about self rather than others; about behaviour rather than appearance; about outsiders rather than family; for possession rather than lack of skill; about opposite rather than same sex.

3. Differences in content occur at the various age levels and according to sex.

4. Twice as many incidents are rejected as accepted; there is an increase in acceptance with age. This is greater for boys than girls. Acceptance score differs according to content.

5. Order of frequency of teasers is—companions, siblings, parents, others.

Conclusion. It is suggested that the basic factor in teasing is a social relationship between teaser and teasee involving individual difference in some characteristic and in status. It is considered therefore to be inherent in social interaction. This would necessitate teaching the child to develop an adaptive attitude toward teasing, namely to accept teasing, to understand individual differences and to be prepared to change behaviour or to accept his own differences.

T39. LAMON, HELEN. A Study of the Colour Selection of Young Children. 1938. Pp. 27.

Problem. To study the colour appreciation of children of Pre-School, Kindergarten, First, and Second Grade age; to investigate colour preferences, developmental differences, and differences relative to specific situations.

Subjects. One hundred and twelve children, 28 at the Institute's Nursery, 84 from Kindergarten, Grades 1 and 2 at Windy Ridge and Bedford Park Public School.

Apparatus. Ninety-six blocks covered with coloured papers, 12 each of red, orange, yellow, green, blue, purple, white, black. Three form boards, neutral grey in colour, each with 5 cut-out spaces. *(a)* rectangular, 9¾ × 9¾ inches, spaces in shape of X; *(b)* rectangular to resemble house 11 inches wide and 11 inches high at peak of roof, spaces for door and three windows; *(c)* rectangular to resemble bus 16¼ inches long × 5¾ inches high, spaces for door and three windows.

Method. The coloured blocks were arranged in a semi-circle in front of the child in eight series, two of each colour to a series.

Each child was asked to choose the blocks he liked best and build with them. Then the form boards were presented singly and he was asked to fit into each the blocks he liked the best.

Results. Nursery school children selected blocks mostly according to position. Older groups selected blocks predominantly on the basis of colour. In these older groups marked preferences were shown for red, blue, and white; purple was markedly not preferred. Individual children did not show marked colour preferences. No significant differences in choices were shown for the different form boards.

Conclusion. 1. Choice by colour in this kind of situation increases with age. 2. No differences in colour preference exist for different situations, but the author suggests that the situations may not have been distinctive enough. 3. Most children at this age tend to choose a variety of colours, beyond the primary colours, without marked individual preference.

T40.   (Ph.D.) LONG, ELEANOR RUTH. A Study of Children's Appreciation of Consequences. 1938. Pp. 51.

Problem. To analyse the development of the appreciation of "consequences" in children of elementary school age.

Discussion. A detailed discussion of learning and discipline is given with an interpretation of Blatz's theory of "consequences." "Learning proceeds in an efficient or inefficient manner depending on the skill with which the learner anticipates the consequences of his behaviour projected into the indefinite future." By increasing the consistency of the consequences of a given action the subject is better able to predict and thus to learn. This establishment of consistent consequences is what is defined as "discipline."

This study limits this total theory to an investigation of how far children of different ages project the consequences of their acts. There are three specific questions: Is the young child sufficiently able to think in terms of consequences to merit the emphasis placed there by our educational theory? Does a genetic pattern show? How does this pattern vary with age, differences in individuals in one school, and differences in schools?

Method. A preliminary study was made with 40 children from six to twelve years at a public school. Individual interviews were arranged during which 25 descriptions of certain situations were given about which the child had to say what he thought would happen next. From these a standard form of procedure, 10 descriptive situations, and a method of analysis and scoring were designed. Examples of the situations are: "Tomorrow is Jack's birthday. What might happen if he has a birthday party?" "George was getting tired of going to school. What might happen if he stops school and looks for a job?"

The responses can be analysed on the following bases: 1. Immediate or remote consequences. 2. Consequences to self or to others. 3. Arbitrary (imposition of authority) or natural (inherent in situation). 4. Pleasant or unpleasant. 5. Single response: multiple response (this—and—this will happen); chain response (this—followed by this—will happen).

The scoring was as follows: *No response* = 0; *Single* = 1; *Multiple* (2 events) = 2; (3 or more) = 3; *Chain* (2 events) = 4; (3 or more) = 5.

INVESTIGATION I

Method. Eight situations were presented individually to 20 six-year-olds, 20 eight-year-olds and 20 ten-year-olds (equal numbers of boys and girls).

Results. 1. As age increases understanding evolves from single consequences (65 per cent of responses of six-year-olds) to multiple (55 per cent of eight-year-olds) to chain (50 per cent of ten-year-olds).

2. The ratios of remote to immediate consequences are six-year-olds .05; eight-year-olds .39 and ten-year-olds .58.

3. The ratios of consequences to self and to others are 6 years .19, 8 years .46 and 10 years .58.

4. The ratios of arbitrary to natural consequences are 6 years .50, 8 years .72, and 10 years .78. However ratio of arbitrary consequences of one's own group to adult authority show the following: 6 years .24, 8 years .37, 10 years .52; showing the child's growing dependence on standards of his peer group.

5. There is no difference with age in ratio of pleasant to unpleasant consequences; however many more (about six times) unpleasant consequences are stated by all groups than are pleasant consequences.

6. On scoring all consequences given by each age group on basis described above the results are as follows:

	Mean	Range
6 years	10.4	5–23
8 years	22.6	9–29
10 years	26.3	19–84

INVESTIGATION II

Method. The same procedure was followed using 43 children from 5 to 8 years old at Windy Ridge School (at which the plan of discipline used was based on the theory of consequences).

Results. These are analysed as in Investigation I and differences between the two groups measured. The total scores of types of consequences given in the results are:

Age	Public School	Windy Ridge
5		13.5
6	10.4	15.1
7		24.2
8	22.6	23.8
10	26.3	

Thus it seems exposure to a form of education in which discipline through understanding consequences plays an important part increased the child's ability to express possible consequences at an earlier age.

As intelligence scores were available for these children correlations were derived between "consequence scores" and there the relationships were M.A. and Consequence Score—.59; C.A. and Consequence Score—.73.

INVESTIGATION III

Method. To compare more carefully the influence of the educational philosophy of discipline 30 children from Windy Ridge were matched with 30 children from a public school (not used in investigation I). The same procedures were followed.

Results. The Windy Ridge children were advanced about one year beyond the public school in their expression of consequences. The consequences they gave were slightly more remote, more concerned with other people, and more influenced by the child's own group.

Special case records on ten children are given in which known factors of home discipline and the child's scores on understanding of consequences are given.

Summary of Results

1. Children as young as five (probably younger) are sufficiently able to think in terms of consequences to merit the emphasis placed there by our educational theory.

2. A pattern of development in the ability to name consequences is evident. As age increases, there are also increases in (a) the frequency of naming remote consequences, (b) of naming consequences to others, (c) of naming consequences springing from the authority of the child's peers. There is no significant trend toward an increase or decrease of pleasant consequences. Unpleasant consequences are more common at all levels. As age increases, the child's understanding of consequences, as measured by his verbalized concepts, follows a definite pattern from single consequences to multiple consequences to chain consequences.

3. Variations of the pattern indicate that older children are better able to give superior responses; more intelligent children are somewhat better able to give superior responses; there is no significant sex differences at these age levels.

4. School training, especially when coupled with adequate home training, increases the child's ability to give superior responses.

Conclusions

1. Experimental data. *(a)* From the responses which children make to problem situations, one may observe a trend to project the consequences of behaviour more and more into the future and also more broadly into the experience of the child. The first of these is represented by an increase of chain responses; and the second by the inclusion of consequences to others as well as to himself and of consequences originating from adults and other children as well as those originating from the physical world. This development is more nearly allied to chronological age than to mental age. This seems to indicate that actual experience is necessary and this trend would indicate the degree of maturity which the individual had attained in habits of learning. *(b)* Skill in anticipating consequences in a more mature fashion is subject to training under an educational technique whereby the individual is permitted to anticipate consequences through his own experience, rather than through values substituted by the expression of arbitrary consequences on the side of the educator. More mature learning habits may be instilled at an earlier age. This can only be brought about by development in the interpretation and evaluation of consequences into the future with reference to time and extent.

2. Theoretical data. In the early stages of development only immediate consequences are perceived and the acquisition of complicated skills is impossible. At this stage the learning may be thought of as predominantly sensory-motor in character but not strictly and exclusively so. Very soon the significance of consequences is appreciated and learning becomes integrated into more complicated patterns. As the significance of the consequences are projected more and more into the future, more complex learning programmes may develop until the time when each act and its consequences is included in the total philosophy of life; at which time the individual may be thought of as a mature, well-integrated personality.

T41. ORD, VIOLET. An Analysis of the Method of Art Instruction Used at the Children's Art Centre, Toronto. 1938. Pp. 30.

Problem. To analyse a specific method of art instruction in terms of *(a)* teaching techniques, *(b)* use of these techniques in teaching with different media, *(c)* accomplishments of pupils under such instruction.

Subjects. Two instructors at the Art Centre; 16 children between the ages of 7 and 9 years.

Setting. Ten art periods were observed, during which the instructors worked on two projects; and two free periods, one occurring before and one after the *second* project. The ten regular periods were at one-week intervals, of one-hour duration.

Method. 1. Verbatim report of instructors' preliminary presentation, and contacts with the individual children during the work period. 2. Detailed description of class organization and the amount and preparation of necessary materials. 3. Each instructor prepared a plan of the project, and after completion, presented a description of the children's achievement and work. 4. A record was kept of the children's work in the two free choice periods and the work compared. 5. Products of the second free period were rated by four art instructors and by pupils' choice.

Results. 1. The main technique employed was suggestion, with specific instruction mainly limited to teaching skill in using materials. 2. Emphasis was placed on general content, leaving child free to choose specific content. 3. Stimulating ideas were given greater emphasis than aesthetic teaching. 4. Work in free period after second project showed definite improvement as compared to work in first free period.

Conclusions 1. The art teachers were interested primarily in fostering children's spontaneous effort, rather than in eliciting finished art products. 2. The medium used limited the child in varying degrees. 3. Guidance is demonstrated as important to maintain the development of skills and to make the child aware of aesthetic qualities as he experiments. 4. Whereas no theme seems needed at nursery school level, with increasing age and ability more limited and more specific themes are needed.

T42. RINTOUL, DOROTHY F. An Experimental Study of Laughter and Smiling in Pre-School Children. 1938. Pp. 25.

Problem. To investigate the influence of age, mental ability, and size of group on laughter and smiling in pre-school children.

Subjects. Seventeen children from Manor Road nursery school. Thirty children from the Institute's Nursery School.

Apparatus. A humorous motion picture eight minutes in length, *Betty Boop.*

Method. 1. 17 children from Manor Road nursery school were shown the film alone five times to determine if there is any practice effect in repeating the same film.

2. 30 children from the Institute's Nursery School were shown the film, first alone, then one with one child, then with two children, with three others, and finally with four others.

Recording. Record sheets divided into 16 half-minute intervals were used. L was entered in each interval that the child laughed; S, smile; and O, neither response.

Results. 1. A very slight decrease in the frequency of laughter and smiling was found when the same film was repeated five times. Rank correlations between laughter on successive occasions were high. 2. When the 23 children who completed the experiment were considered as a whole, it was found that the frequency of laughter and smiling increased as the size of the group was progressively increased. There were, however, individual differences from this trend. 3. Laughter and age correlated $+.19$; mental age $+.34$; I.Q. $+.44$. 4. Amount of laughter evoked during each half minute was analysed but seemed difficult to interpret in terms of the story content.

Conclusions. 1. Most pre-school children laugh and smile more with other children than they do when alone. 2. Amount of laughter is not related to age, mental ability, or sex.

T43.   SPARLING, MARGARET. Variation and Predictive Value of the Intelligence Quotients of Pre-School Children. 1938. Pp. 24.

Problem. To what extent can the I.Q.'s of pre-school children be used to predict their I.Q.'s at a later date?

Subjects. Seventy-two children between the ages of 2 and 7 years who up to the age of 5 years attended the Institute's Nursery School. The average I.Q. of this group at 7 years of age was 122.

Material. A series of intelligence test scores for children between 2 and 7 years were obtained during their attendance at the Nursery School twice yearly, and after graduation once a year. Tests used— Kuhlmann, Merrill-Palmer, Stanford-Binet.

Method. Results from these tests were analysed to show. 1. Differences between I.Q. distributions at different age levels. 2. Differences in variation of I.Q. between 2 and 7, 3 and 7, 4 and 7 years. 3. Variation related to size of I.Q. 4. Variation related to earlier and later tests. 5. The accuracy with which pre-school tests predict I.Q.'s at 7.

Results. On the basis of four or five test scores at yearly intervals for the 72 children it was found: 1. The average I.Q. at 2 years is 108, at 3 years 123, at 4 years 126 and at 7 years 122. 2. The I.Q.'s at the three-year-old level show the greatest range. 3. The I.Q. at 7 years is predicted more accurately by the I.Q. at 4, than from those obtained at 2 or 3 years of age. 4. Lower I.Q.'s obtained at the early age levels show a greater increase at 7 years, than do the higher I.Q.'s. 5. The prediction of an I.Q. at 7 from an I.Q. at 2, 3, or 4 is extremely unreliable. For example, the I.Q.'s obtained at 3 years varied over a range of 82 points at the seven-year-old level.

Conclusions. 1. Very little reliance can be placed on an I.Q. of pre-school years as an indication of what it will be during school years. 2. With "above average" children, such as this group, it may be expected that on the whole their early I.Q.'s are lower than they will be later. 3. It is suggested from this study that the I.Q.'s at early ages are being influenced by outside psychological factors and that it would be valuable to investigate these factors and their influence. (M. S.)

T44. STEWART, MARGARET C. The Application of a Theory of Discipline in a Private Home Setting. 1938. Pp. 55.

Problem. This study was arranged to test whether it was possible to incorporate into a home the basic principles of child training, applied in a nursery school, without "institutionalizing" the home.

Subjects. Two boys aged 5 and 3 years (I.Q.'s 115, 119 respectively) observed in their own home over a period of 12 weeks, during which time a careful plan of child training was followed under the guidance of a resident student.

The philosophy of discipline employed was the same as in the Nursery School at the Institute of Child Study. Both boys presented problems of maladjustment in the home and this study was incidental to the therapeutic interest involved in the training programme.

Method. Records were kept on both children for 90 days. 1. Non-compliance, i.e. refusal to co-operate in routine. 2. Discipline, i.e. when adult introduced an extrinsic consequence. 3. Emotional episodes. 4. Running diary, i.e. covering routine activities.

Results. 1. There was a decrease in non-compliant behaviour in both children when the first six weeks were compared with the second six weeks, especially with reference to physical resistance. 2. A decrease in extrinsic disciplinary procedure was noted for both children, especially with the older boy. 3. A marked decrease in emotional episodes, especially with respect to quarrelling, was noted in both children. 4. There was a gradual acceptance of responsibility by both children of routine requirements.

Conclusions. This indicates that the programme of discipline used in the Nursery School can be effectively incorporated into home training.

B5. BLATZ, WILLIAM E. *The Five Sisters: A Study of Child Psychology.* Toronto: McClelland and Stewart, 1938. Pp. 209.

A popular book with its factual material derived from M11. The plan of training used with the "quints" and their responses to it are described and interpreted for the lay reader.

The Bulletin of the Institute of Child Study, University of Toronto, BERNHARDT, KARL S. (ed.) 1938–

Known at first as the *Parent Education Bulletin,* this magazine has been published quarterly since 1938 under the editorship of Dr. Bernhardt and a committee of the staff. Its purpose is to present "the interpretation and practical application of the current findings in the fields of child study and parent education." Its fiftieth number will be published simultaneously with this book.

1939

T45. BERTRAM, VIRGINIA. A Study of Affective Behaviour in Eight Pre-School Children. 1939. Pp. 40.

Problem. To study in detail the individual differences in affective behaviour of 8 three-year-old children. The specific forms of behaviour studied were (a) emotional—crying and extreme resistance or aggression; (b) mild affective—facial and vocal expression which seemed indicative of heightened feeling.

Subjects. Eight children ranging in age from 3 years 2 months to 3 years 8 months, attending the Institute Nursery School. These children were selected from a group of 31 on the basis of age and good attendance.

Setting. "Emotional" behaviour was observed as it occurred throughout the Nursery School day in all situations. "Mild affective" behaviour was observed in the outdoor free play period of the nursery school.

Method. "Emotional" behaviour was recorded daily for each child from the time he entered school for from 12 to 17 months. "Mild affective" behaviour was observed for eight 15-minute periods for each child over a period of four months, and also at the end of the observational period.

Recording. "Emotional" behaviour was recorded on prepared forms by the Nursery School staff as a part of the regular Nursery School recording system. Objective details were noted. "Mild affective" behaviour and details re the accompanying situation were recorded by an observer as they took place.

Results. 1. Seven types of "emotional" behaviour were recorded. 2. Seven types of situation causing emotional behaviour were recorded. 3. Fifteen types of vocal and sixteen types of facial behaviour were recorded under "mild affective" behaviour. 4. More individual difference than group similarity was shown throughout. The following differences were noted: (*a*) Differences in frequency and type of "emotional" behaviour in frequency change with age; (*b*) Difference in the type of causal situation and the change of causal situation with age; (*c*) Difference in the frequency and the type of "mild affective" behaviour; (*d*) Difference in the relationship of "emotional" to "mild affective" behaviour.

Conclusion. The need for further study of an experimental nature in order to understand the meaning of individual differences in affective behaviour is emphasized.

T46. CATES, TANNIS. A Study of the Dominative and Submissive Behaviour of Eight Pre-School Children. 1939. Pp. 25.

Problem. To study the incidence of dominant and submissive behaviour and their consistency of appearance from one setting to another. (Dominance is defined as behaviour when a child either attempts to direct or control or to resist or non-comply; submission is defined as giving another child opportunity to direct or control or being compliant to direction and control.)

Subjects. Eight children (5 girls and 3 boys) of 3 years 3 months to 3 years 6 months, in attendance at the Institute's Nursery School for at least one year.

Apparatus. Two settings free play period in Nursery School playground, 32 children in attendance; experimental situation—teetertotter placed in separate room without other equipment.

Method. Each child was observed for 6 fifteen-minute periods during free play period over 3 months and for 7 fifteen-minute periods in experimental setting. In free setting there was no control of activity; in the experimental setting each child was paired with one of the other 7 children of the experimental group and the pair was directed towards activity with the teeter-totter. Recording was by category as follows—initiated and responded contacts; playing alone; watching; parallel activity; co-operative play. One notation was made at fifteen-second intervals.

Results. 1. In both settings incidents of dominant behaviour are markedly more frequent than submissive behaviour for all children but ratios show considerable individual difference. 2. Commands are most frequently used type of dominance. 3. The group complies more than it resists dominance and each child is more successful than unsuccessful with his dominant behaviour. 4. Little relationship is shown between amount of dominant and submissive behaviour divided into initiated and response types. 5. Individual ratios tend to approximate each other in the two settings. 6. Individually, the children differ in degree of success irrespective of type of dominance used and each child shows an individually different pattern in the frequency of appearance of the various types of behaviour; also a difference in behaviour with different children.

Conclusions. 1. The marked predominance of dominant behaviour in these pre-school children suggests a developmental stage in learning social skill at which other methods of contact have not been acquired. 2. Individual differences suggest that each child's behaviour is dependent upon factors other than age and environmental situation. 3. That the results are consistent in the two settings indicates that the characteristics of dominant and submissive behaviour reflect a general characteristic of social behaviour irrespective of the particular situation.

Comment. This study is an interesting fore-runner of present studies on group dynamics and interrelationships between individuals.

T47. (Ph.D.) MASON, MOLLY. Changes in the Galvanic Skin Response Accompanying Reports of Changes in Meaning During Oral Repetition. 1939. Pp. 124.

T48. MILES, HAZEL. A Study of Responsibility in a Nursery School Setting. 1939. Pp. 47.

Problem. To study responsibility as it appears in a group of nursery school children with reference to *(a)* clarifying objective criteria for evaluating responsibility; *(b)* determining whether responsibility appears as a general characteristic of a child's behaviour; *(c)* attempting a measurement of developmental level; *(d)* clarifying types of behaviour that indicate lack of responsibility.

Subjects. Three boys and five girls, age range 3 years 2 months to 3 years 8 months, who attended the Nursery School of the Institute for one year.

Setting. Observations were taken in seven Nursery School situations—morning water; toilet; washing; dressing; eating; sleeping; and indoor play.

Method. 1. Each child was observed ten times in each of the six routines over a four months' period. Items recorded were *(a)* Initial Act—whether self initiated; *(b)* Frequency of promptings; *(c)* Behaviour necessitating prompting—dawdling; over-social behaviour; doing nothing; irrelevant behaviour; *(d)* Verbalization; *(e)* Time taken; *(f)* Pertinent information.

2. Observation of Play—two separate 20-minute periods taken during last month of observation. Items recorded were *(a)* Initial act; *(b)* Material used; *(c)* Type of activity at minute intervals (watching, passive, active, routine, manipulative, constructive use); *(d)* Child's comments; *(e)* Adult relationships.

Results. 1. The group have few promptings in initial act. 2. The children differ individually in the frequency of promptings throughout; in the behaviour giving rise to prompting and in the situations in which most prompting occurs. 3. The behaviour requiring prompting differs in any one child from situation to situation. 4. Each child shows a consistency in behaviour throughout the situations shown by ranking the children according to frequency of promptings. 5. The group have few promptings in play and spend most time in constructive use of materials. 6. Individual differences in pattern of play are evident. In general those showing longer time in constructive play change less frequently, and have less prompting. 7. A comparison of behaviour in routine and play shows a tendency for those children having fewer promptings in routine to show the same behaviour in play; also to play constructively for longer and have less changes.

Conclusions. Degree of responsibility can be measured in a nursery school setting in terms of the relative number of promptings; length of time spent in constructive play, and frequency of changing activity in play; so defined it is suggested that responsibility is a generalized feature of the child's activity appearing in Routine and Play, e.g. the child who has learned to accept responsibility in his routine shows self direction in his play.

T49.   SCOTT, FRANCES. Adult-Child Relationships in a Nursery School
       Setting. 1939. Pp. 32.

Problem. To investigate adult-child relationships in a nursery
school setting.

Subjects. The subjects observed were eight children between the
ages of 3 years and 2 months, and 3 years and 8 months, who attended
the Institute's Nursery School, and six members of the staff.

Method. Verbatim records of the verbal contacts between these
adults and children were recorded in two routine and two play
situations. These contacts were classified into categories under adult
and child initiated contacts.

Results. Three general types of contacts were found both for the
children and the adults. All of the children initiated these three types,
i.e. asking for help, asking or giving personal information, and
initiating purely social contacts, but they differed in the degree to
which they used these modes of approach to the adults. The adults
contacted all the children for purposes of giving direction, "personal
interest," and social conversation. The greatest percentage of the
adult contacts were in the form of direction, "suggestions" being used
more often than "statements," showing that the adults usually contact
the children when they feel it is necessary but not otherwise.

It was found that the greatest percentage of contacts, both child
and adult initiated, occurred during the routines, thus leaving the
child free during the play periods to assume responsibility for his own
behaviour. In the routines the adult assumed the role of a teacher,
helping the child.

Interpretations of the above results have shown individual differences in the relations of these eight children with the adults. (F. S.)

1940

T50.   MACKAY, CAROLINE. A Study of the Understanding of Arbitrary
       Consequences by Pre-School children. 1940. Pp. 26.

Problem. To discover children's interpretations of nursery school
situations in which arbitrary consequences are administered.

Subjects. Twelve girls and 6 boys between 3.4 years and 4.8 years
of age from the Institute Nursery School.

Apparatus. A stage with miniature reproductions of the playground and playroom at the Nursery School was constructed. Puppets 2 inches high were made to represent the "adult" and two children. Twelve pantomimes representing situations in nursery school life (e.g. child walking up slide followed by adult taking him as a consequence to sit on chair).

Method. After preliminary play with the equipment each child was taken to observe a "pantomime." In all, 12 situations each about ten minutes in length were presented to each child. (No child observed more than two of these in any one week.) The child was shown each situation twice and immediately asked why the consequence had occurred—one definite question for all children followed each situation, this was followed by questions directed to the particular child's response. (Detailed diagrams of the equipment and a complete outline of the procedure is given in the Appendix.)

Results. 1. There were 216 responses; 19 per cent were inadequate; 1 per cent explained the discipline on basis of adult authority; 26 per cent on the basis of "wrongness" of the behaviour; 54 per cent on the basis of not meeting natural requirements.

2. The author considers the last three types of response indicative of three levels of maturity; she finds the most mature level of response (e.g. not meeting natural requirements) occurs most frequently in situations involving incorrect social behaviour and misuse of materials and least in situations involving danger. There were wide individual differences in the frequency with which these more highly mature answers were given by different children. Their frequency correlated .73 with I.Q. and .64 with M.A.

3. The maturity of replies was related to actual number of disciplinary episodes recorded for the child during the previous two years. The six children giving least number of mature replies had 44 disciplinary episodes; the six giving most number of mature answers had 16. The correlation between maturity of answers and staff's rating of the child's adequacy of behaviour was +.61. Thus maturity of understanding of consequences and behaviour adjustment are related.

Conclusions. Children interpreted disciplinary consequences depicted in a puppet pantomime as an expression of adult authority, as "wrongness of behaviour," or as failure to meet necessary requirements. The most mature interpretation was related to M.A. and I.Q. and to the child's actual conformity in school. Thus it is concluded children are able to recognize the mature meaning of disciplinary consequences.

Comment. This thesis gives a concise statement of the philosophy of discipline used in the Institute's Nursery School. (Compare with T40 and T17.)

T51. REA, JOCELYN. A Systematic Evaluation of the Content of Pre-School Stories in Terms of Children's Recalls. 1940. Pp. 36.

Problem. (a) To make a systematic analysis of the content of selected stories for pre-school children. (b) To analyse children's "recalls" as a basis for determining what constitutes a good story for pre-school children.

Theory. A clear and concise statement of the relation of stories to general principles of child development is given. On the basis of this it is assumed that what a child recalls of a story will depend on what he has attended to, which will be the "interest" of the material. On measures of recall, judgments of the "goodness" of the story are based.

Subjects. Twelve girls from the Institute and Windy Ridge Nursery 4.0 to 4.9 years of age.

Material. From a recommended list of 50 stories, 12 were selected on the basis of being unfamiliar to the children and as representing a wide range of different characteristics.

Method. Each child was read a story and asked to tell the story back to the adult; the adult wrote her recall verbatim. At the next period the child was shown a typescript of her recall and told she could have it to take home. The order of the stories was rotated with different children. (A detailed account of the material is given and is useful in showing how experimental procedure can be adapted for young children.)

Results. 1. The stories were analysed according to verbal content into 8 categories and according to content and the children's recalls by verbal content (a) same as the story, (b) additional to the story; and by ideational content. 2. The recalls were compared with the original story on the above basis. 3. The verbal categories which differentiated the stories to the greatest extent were description, objects, and action verbs. 4. The recalls showed more retention of characters, objects, and action verbs than any other criteria. 5. Plots were occasionally recalled but "morals" never.

Conclusion. "A short story with few characters having simple action constantly repeated, presented directly with little description, is best recalled by the children and hence the one in which they are most interested."

An outline of the factors to be taken into account in the construction of children's stories is given.

Comment. Although the author is concerned chiefly with developing a method for analysing stories and children's recalls of them, several hints are given indicating the dynamics of children's memories, which follow the principles enumerated by Bartlett,[6] and suggest an approach by which the study of memory schemata in the young child could be studied.

T52.   TURNER, KATHLEEN. An Analysis of Imitative Behaviour in Relation to Learning. 1940. Pp. 31.

Problem. To investigate certain aspects of imitation as it occurs in a learning situation, *(a)* comparing efficiency of learning with and without the possibility of imitation; *(b)* investigating the "type" of imitation used in a learning situation.

Subjects. Fifteen children 3 to 4 years of age from a day nursery were divided into three equated groups. Each sub-group was presented the form-boards and situations in different order. A group of five children, a year older than the subjects, were used in the imitation situations as demonstrators, "Imitatees."

Apparatus. Three different sets of two similar form-boards to be completed with twelve blocks. These were similar to the Merrill-Palmer Intelligence test form-boards.

Method. 1. Each child was presented individually with the problem of putting the blocks into the board. 2. The following situations were used: *(a)* the child worked alone (alone); *(b)* the child worked in a room with an imitatee (imitation); *(c)* the child worked with adult guidance (adult). 3. Two test situations which were repetitions of 2 *(a)* were given. 4. Each child was observed for 15 five-minute periods. Three trial periods were given in each situation, followed by the first test situation. The second test situation was six weeks later. 5. Prepared record forms were used to note correct and incorrect placements of blocks. Imitative behaviour was defined as a child perform-

[6]F. C. Bartlett, *Remembering—A Study in Experimental and Social Psychology* (Cambridge: 1932).

ance of an act which appeared to be stimulated by observation of behaviour of the imitatee.

Results. Performance in each situation was scored on basis of four criteria based on types of errors. Results on the three situations as they occurred and on the tests were compared.

1. *Comparison of Performance in Situations 1 and 2.* Performance in imitation situations was superior and there was more prolonged interest and greater attention. Test performance (in situations 4 and 5) was superior after imitation situations.

2. *Comparison of Performance in Situations 2 and 3.* Performance in the imitation situation was superior to the situation with adult help. Similarly the test situation following imitation showed superior performance.

3. *Analysis of Imitative Behaviour.* Frequency of imitative behaviour decreased as form board proficiency increased. Imitation occurred when the child was experiencing the greatest difficulty.

Conclusions. 1. In a situation with imitation, form-board performance is superior to the performance in a situation without imitation. 2. In a situation with imitation, learning is more rapid than in a situation without imitation. 3. The test performance following a situation with imitation is superior to the test performance following a situation without imitation. 4. In a situation with imitation, attentive adjustment is greater than in a situation without imitation. 5. The imitative behaviour that occurred during this experiment is purposeful.

M13. BLATZ, W. E., BERNHARDT, KARL S., MILLICHAMP, DOROTHY A., JOHNSON, FRANCES L., FOSTER, NAN. *Outlines for Parent Education Groups, Discipline.* Child Development Series No. 17. Toronto: University of Toronto Press. 1940. Pp. 57.

The plan of discipline suggested in this outline has been in use for the last twenty-five years and its efficacy has been substantiated in research studies (e.g. T11, T40, T54) and the daily programme of the Nursery School.

M14. NORTHWAY, MARY L. Appraisal of the Social Development of Children at a Summer Camp. Univ. of Toronto, Psych. Series. Vol. 5, no. 1., 1940. Pp. 63.

This is the first Toronto publication using sociometric techniques. A scoring method was introduced by which social relationships among 80 children were measured on the basis of their expressed choice of

companion for a variety of situations. The sociometric structure of
the camp was defined and changes in the social status and relations
of a child during a three-week interval appraised.

M15. SALTER, MARY D. *An Evaluation of Adjustment Based upon
      the Concept of Security.* Child Development Series No. 18.
      Toronto: University of Toronto Press, 1940. Pp. 72.

This is the first published statement on the concept of *security*
which has come to form a major part of the thinking and research of
the Institute.

The author gives a detailed analysis of the concept stating that
"security is essentially a subjective experience," implying the "immediate experience of adequacy in any given situation" and a "feeling
of adequacy to meet future consequences." An individual's security
may be appraised in four areas of life (1) social intimacies—familial
and extra-familial; (2) philosophy of life; (3) vocational adjustment
(work); (4) avocational adjustment (leisure). The author constructs
scales by which security in familial and extra-familial social intimacies
may be measured.

This investigation has proposed the concept of security as a basis
of evaluating the adjustment of the individual, has outlined a methodology for devising a means of such evaluation, and has subjected
these to empirical test within two significant fields of adjustment.
Considered as the first step of a more extensive investigation this
study may be said to represent a test-case in which the practicality
of the proposed method of evaluation has been established.

B6. BLATZ, W. E. *Hostages to Peace: Parents and the Children of
     Democracy.* New York: Morrow, 1940. Pp. 208.

Written in the form of a series of letters to an intelligent American
mother, this book interprets the Institute's philosophy in the context
of problems prevalent in 1940, at the outbreak of the Second World
War.

In succinct style, interwoven with many homely examples, the
author's interpretation of instincts, emotion, discipline, and education
are presented. The book also contains the Director's first published
statement on Security (pp. 181f) (Cp. M15).

The author's own summary reads:

War is not an instinct. There are no social instincts. Human beings have
more to learn than any other species. Education, and not propaganda or
censorship, is the ideal directive method.

The emotions are useful, enjoyable and thrilling experiences. It is only through lack of education or faulty direction that fear and anger become devastating and disintegrating experiences.

Discipline is a plan of education which depends on a rational arrangement of consequences rather than upon punishment, retaliation or sentiment. Suggestions are more effective than force, and patience more efficient than commands. The chief aim of education is the development of human values which will contribute to, rather than make demands upon, community life.

Security is the only healthy goal in life. Safety is dangerous. Insecurity makes for progress; but if the individual does not accept the challenge of insecurity, then he finds it necessary to adopt some form of compensation. These compensatory mechanisms are the root of all social turbulences, of which was is the most disgraceful and unnecessary.[7]

B7. NORTHWAY, MARY L. (ed.) *Charting the Counselor's Course: A Guide for Camp Leaders.* Toronto: Longmans, Green, 1940. Pp. vii + 118.

1941

1942

T53. HAROLD, ELSIE F. An Analysis of the Success of Methods of Initiating Social Contacts by Young Children. 1942. Pp. 32.

Problem. To investigate the relative success of various methods four-year-old children use to initiate social contacts.

Subjects. Thirteen children ranging from 4 years to 4 years 10 months, Institute of Child Study.

Method. 1. Each child was observed for ten minutes as he entered or re-entered the playground. This was repeated eight times, not more frequently than twice a week. Observations of the child's initial contacts were entered descriptively on a prepared record form (shown in appendix). 2. Each child was taken individually to a similar but unfamiliar nursery school and his contacts observed for one period of 30 minutes (Hillcrest Progressive School).

Results. 1. Of the 271 contacts observed 38 per cent were judged to be successful (i.e. a relationship was established) and 62 per cent unsuccessful. (Criterion of success was that of Mallay.[8]) 2. The contacts were classified into 24 types of behaviour and the success and

---

[7]Reprinted by permission of William Morrow and Company, Inc., New York.
[8]H. Mallay. "A study of some of the factors underlying the establishment of social contacts at the preschool level" (*Jr. of Genetic Psychology*, 1935, Vol. 47, pp. 431-457).

failure of each type analysed. 3. An analysis of types of contact used by individual subjects was made and compared with their rank on total successes. From this patterns of social behaviour were developed.

Conclusion. 1. The four-year-olds' most frequent form of initiating contacts was by using "co-operative" behaviour. Asking for co-operation was used more frequently than offering co-operation. 2. Co-operative behaviour is more successful in establishing a relationship than non-co-operative. The "giving" type is more successful than the "asking" type. 3. There are individual differences in the extent and type of behaviour used and in the success of it. 4. Four distinguishable types of behaviour are described. The author suggests that the adequacy or inadequacy of children's behaviour in social situations is one of the best indices of their general security.

1943

T54. GREGORY, MARION. A Study of Children's Behaviour with Chosen Companions in an Experimental Play Setting. 1943. Pp. 38.

Problem. To investigate the factors operating in the selection of companions at the three- and four-year-old level. (The assumption was that if the subjects were allowed to choose their companions with reference to an interesting situation, observation of their behaviour would indicate in what way the subjects derived satisfaction in those particular relationships.

Subjects. The subjects were 14 children attending the Institute's Nursery School. They ranged in chronological age from 3 years, 2 months, to 4 years, 10 months.

Material. The apparatus consisted of a large set of new brightly coloured blocks and two trucks arranged in a familiar room from which other obvious distractions had been eliminated.

Method. The subject was taken from a free play situation to look at books alone with the experimenter. He was then told he was going to play with some new blocks and was asked to choose another child to accompany him. The two children and experimenter then proceeded to the "block room" where the children were told they could build whatever they wished. The experimenter sat near by and kept verbatim records of their conversation. Observations were made in a series of four intervals of ten minutes in length over a 10-week period.

The verbatim records were analysed for qualitative differences in the roles assumed by the subjects.

Results. The selected child exceeded the chooser more often than the chooser exceeded the selected child in 14 categories in which were included such qualities of behaviour as amount of talking, number of new ideas expressed, amount of interpretive conversation, amount of directive conversation. In three categories, namely, repetition of other child's conversation, appropriation of other child's ideas, and submission to other's suggestions the chooser exceeded the selected child more often. Although this consistent trend of difference in behaviour was apparent, the extent of difference was slight. Objective factors of sex, chronological age, and mental age did not seem to influence choice. The range in number of times subjects were chosen was from 0–9.

Conclusion. Within the limits set by this study the following conclusions were reached as to the factors operating in the three- and four-year-old's choice of companion. The subjects tended to choose play companions who slightly exceeded them in talking, contributing to the block construction, taking the initiative, and attempting control of the situation. The choosers usually exhibited a submissive attitude to the companion's directions. There were consistent individual differences in pattern of behaviour in the experimental setting.

Comment. This is a precursor to studies of the interaction of subjects of known sociometric relation, in progress at present. (M. G.)

B10. BERNHARDT, K. S. *Elementary Psychology.* Toronto: The Life Underwriters Association of Canada, 1943. Pp. 300.

1944

T55. FRANKEL, ESTHER B. The Social Relationships of Pre-School Children. 1944. Pp. 85.

Problem. To compare sociometric and observational methods for measuring the social relationships of young children.

To discover some of the factors related to children's social relationships.

Subjects. Twenty-three three-and four-year-olds at the Institute's Nursery School.

Method. 1. A specially adapted form of the sociometric test (3 criteria) was given individually to the children. Scored by Northway's

(weighted) and Bronfenbrenner's (unweighted) method R = .98.
2. Challman's method of observing children playing together outside
was used and 65 records obtained. From these: Play contact scores
(total number of contacts each child received) and Friendship indices
(number of contacts between two particular children).

Results. 1. Sociometric scores and play contact scores correlated
+.45; thus the two scales do not measure the identical phenomena but
two aspects of social relationships. Sociometric acceptability determined by others' preference for one is not the same as actual acceptance which is determined by the fluctuating structure of the group.
2. A child actually plays with more children than he verbally chooses
on the sociometric test. Actual social contacts are wider than stated
preferences. 3. Playground "friendships" (measured by Friendship
Index) and sociometric reciprocal choices show a consistency of 60
per cent. 4. Factors related to social relationships: *(a)* Age is not
related to sociometric status but shows a correlation of +.60 with play
contacts. Neither I.Q. nor number of days of absence had any relation
to sociometric status. *(b)* Sociometric scores and play contact scores
were related to number of discipline and emotional episodes as
recorded in the routine records. The sociometric score was high when
both the emotional and discipline scores were high; the play contact
scores were high when the discipline scores were high, but low when
the emotional scores were high. *(c)* When "friends" were examined
there seemed to be a balance between high and low emotional scores
in the relationships.

Comment. This study was the first introduction of sociometry into
the Institute's Nursery School and has formed the basis of the present
twice-yearly sociometric testing. (Published 1947. See entry M17.)

B8. BLATZ, WILLIAM E. *Understanding the Young Child.* Toronto:
Clarke, Irwin, 1944. Pp. 278.

This is the most recent statement of the Institute's understanding
of child development. Written for parents and nursery workers, it
provides systematic statements of the concepts of learning, discipline,
and security and outlines the processes of social development,
imagery, and imagination; the complementary roles of the nursery
school and the home in the child's education are discussed.

The author's own description of this book is as follows:

Herein is a brief outline of the way children grow up and how they may
be influenced. It makes no pretensions toward infallibility. The data in
child psychology at the present day are still too new, too attenuated, and

too undigested for such an attitude. On the other hand, in a book of this nature there may be an excuse for dogmatism. For the sake of clarity, the author has been dogmatic. Subsequent study may prove a good deal stated within these pages to be inaccurate; it would be surprising if such were not the case. But the book presents a system which at least holds together fairly well. Some of the "products" of this system have already reached maturity, and at present it can be safely said that no harm has come to them—nor to society through them. Furthermore, they seem to have enjoyed their infancy, childhood, and youth. (p. 14)[9]

B9. FLETCHER, MARGARET I. and DENISON, MARGARET CONBOY. *The High Road of Song for Nursery Schools and Kindergartens.* With a foreword by W. E. Blatz and introduction by Dorothy A. Millichamp. Toronto: Gage, 1944. Pp. xii + 124.

A collection of nursery rhymes, songs, singing games, and playlets based on practical "research" with children's music at the Institute's Nursery School.

1945

T56. GRAHAM, MARY B. Interests of Five, Six and Seven-year-old Children. 1945. Pp. 28.

Problem. To study the interests of children 5 to 7. (This was undertaken because relatively little information appeared in literature and as an attempt to answer some of the difficulties arising in the supervision of the Dominion-Provincial Junior Day Care Programme which had recently been inaugurated.)

Subjects. Two groups of 43 children each, ranging in age from 5 years 0 months to 7 years 8 months. One group was from Windy Ridge Day School, the other from Forest Hill South Preparatory School. All the children were from similar backgrounds and within the normal range of intelligence.

Materials. 1. Questionnaire composed of seven simple, direct questions, requiring definite answers, about the child's play activity and interests. 2. Three picture books: There were twelve pictures in each of the three following books: *(a)* adult occupations and interests; *(b)* children's play, *(c)* objects from everyday life.

Method. The play activities of the children were investigated by two methods. One consisted in observing each subject as he looked through books of pictures representing a variety of play activities.

[9]Reprinted by permission of the publishers: University of London Press Ltd., London, England; Clarke, Irwin & Company Limited, Toronto; and William Morrow & Company, Inc., New York.

Interest in the activities was determined by timing how long a subject looked at each of the pictures. The other method was that of asking each subject to report what he did, or would like to do, outside of school hours.

Results. There was a wide variation in interests as expressed by five-, six-, and seven-year-old children. The interests of these children were easily captivated by the pictures which were presented first. In spite of the fact that these children have few crystallized interests, they did show an interest in policemen, farms, sand, dolls, skipping, boats, houses, fire engines, trains, and unusual pattern designs.

Conclusions. Because there are few crystallized interests there is a great opportunity for the Junior Day Care centres to introduce a variety of experiences and materials to these children. From these may be formed a background out of which a child, in a later stage of his growth, may develop his special interests. (M.B.G.)

1946

A3. FRANKEL, ESTHER. "The Social Relationships of Nursery School Children." *Sociometry*, 1946, IX, 210-225.

T57. McKENZIE, DOROTHY. Patterns of Problem-Solving of the Pre-School Child and the Influence of Instruction on These Patterns. 1946. Pp. 22.

Problem. To study the qualitative learning patterns of pre-school children and to compare the influence of instruction and non-instruction on these patterns.

Subjects. Two matched groups of children, 15 in each group, varying in age from 2 years 1 month to 4 years 9 months; average age 3 years 7 months for each group; average M.A. 4–4 and 4–2. All children were at the Institute's Nursery School.

Apparatus. A board 11½ × 18½ inches standing vertically; 7 steel pins 2 inches apart horizontally; one pin 1/100-inch smaller than the others was in third position. A toothbrush could be hung on this pin only. The difference in size of the third pin did not appear to be perceptually recognized by children of this age.

Method. Each child was tested five times; the tests were spaced at one-week, two-week, three-week, four-week and five-week intervals. The child was brought individually to the test room and shown the equipment. Group A (uninstructed) was told "to take the toothbrush and find the nail it went on." Group B was shown which nail the toothbrush fitted and then told to put it on the right nail. In later trials both groups were told—"Here is the toothbrush; you put it on the right nail."

A prepared record chart enabled the pattern the child followed to be recorded. The errors and length of time were recorded.

Results. 1. Quantitative. The amount of time and number of errors were not significantly different between the two groups. Errors did not relate to C.A. and only +.3 with M.A.

2. Qualitative. From charting the detail of the child's activities on each trial it was found that *(a)* more children in the uninstructed group use "systematic" patterns (i.e. one with an apparent plan), *(b)* the older child uses more "systematic" patterns.

Conclusions. 1. Instruction did not accelerate learning. 2. Older children used systematic patterns more frequently than younger ones. 3. The uninstructed group used more systematic patterns than the instructed group.

T58. NICHOLSON, JEAN G. The Records of the Institute of Child Study with Special Reference to the Follow-up Interview. 1946. Pp. 51.

Problem. To investigate critically the methods being used to record the data for a longitudinal study of individual development in progress at the Institute, as follows: 1. To study recording methods now in use. 2. To evaluate data on these records by means of analysis of sample records. 3. To experiment with new devices in obtaining data.

Subjects. 1. Records of 149 individuals who attended Nursery School at the Institute. 2. Records of thirty-three of these Nursery School graduates with follow-up records at ages 9, 12, and 15 years. 3. Interviews with twenty-two of the above subjects (in 2) who were 16 years of age or over.

Materials. 1. The cumulative records of the Institute of Child Study kept since 1926. 2. Yearly interview record forms.

Method. 1. Data on the development and present organization of the recording system were obtained from articles and from staff members. 2. A summary sheet was devised for facilitating organization of information at the three age levels selected for study. A study was made of the number of times information was lacking in the original records. Two topics, I.Q. variation, and change in ambition, were isolated for detailed study. 3. An experimental interview form was constructed including—direct questions about nursery schools and interviews per se, cards with pictures indicating interests to be rated, a list of questions concerning behaviour problems of children. An interview was conducted individually with the 22 graduates using this form.

Results. 1. Many inadequacies of the interview form were shown. The summary form was shown to be a valuable tool for tabulating raw data. The records were shown to be valuable for specific studies such as I.Q. variation and change in ambition. 2. The ranking of cards provided information which could be analysed in both a quantitative and qualitative way. The questions concerning behaviour problems drew forth a wide variety of responses; indicated a variety of attitudes.

Conclusions. 1. The present recording system could be improved by *(a)* appointment of a "Director" to integrate individual records into a system; *(b)* keeping a record of revisions and additions to the system. 2. The interview form could be improved by *(a)* re-organization of listed topics; *(b)* more careful attention to record keeping by the interviewer. Information contained in the present records is adequate for many forms of analysis. 3. The new devices appeared to break the monotony of the long interview. The ranking method if used for objective data previously acquired in a less precise way would facilitate comparison of individuals. It was felt that some indirect method of gaining insight into attitudes (such as the one used here) would be a valuable addition to the recording system. (J.G.P.)

Comment. Many of these suggestions have been incorporated into the developmental recording system at the Institute.

T59. SMITH, SHIRLEY. A Comparison of Separate and Combined Playgrounds for Juniors and Seniors in Nursery Schools. 1946. Pp. 38.

Problem. This study was an attempt to answer a question raised particularly by the establishment of Dominion-Provincial Wartime Day Nurseries regarding the desirability of common or separate outdoor play space or periods in a nursery school programme for junior and senior age groups.

Method. The author studied six government day nurseries; in two of these the juniors and seniors were combined in one playground; in two separated, and in two separated in the morning and combined in the afternoon periods. Other factors about the nurseries were kept as constant as possible, e.g. length of time of operation, number of children, number of staff, etc. Evaluations were based on (1) number of emotional episodes; (2) number of adult interferences as reported by the supervisor; (3) descriptive records of play and social groupings made by the writer.

Results and Conclusions. 1. There was no difference in number of emotional episodes for seniors on combined or separate playgrounds. Juniors have slightly fewer episodes in the combined setting. 2. There was no difference in frequency of adult interference with seniors in the two settings. The adult interferes more frequently with juniors in the combined setting. 3. There was little difference in amount of social play of seniors or juniors in the two situations.

Comment. The main contribution of this thesis lies in the fact it clearly shows the many difficulties there are in attempting to evaluate a practical situation on the basis of psychological evidence. Although the carefully conducted observations and recording show no great difference between the situations on any of the criteria used, the writer's considered opinions in interpreting the findings in the light of her own practical nursery experiences led her to suggest that separate playgrounds are more desirable for juniors and for increasing the adequacy of adult supervision. Excellent diagrams of the lay-outs of the six playgrounds are given.

M16. NORTHWAY, M. L. Studies in the Field of Sociometry, a series of lectures summarizing the Toronto Studies. Toronto: University of Toronto Press, 1946. Pp. 36 + appendix (mimeo).

B11. POPPLETON, MARJORIE. *Where's Patsy?* Toronto: Oxford, 1936. A story and picture book for the pre-school child.

1947

T60. GATCH, HELEN L. A Comparison of Learning in a Museum with Learning in a School. 1947. Pp. 33.

Problem. To compare the learning of Grade 6 children taught by means of a museum excursion with that of an equivalent group taught at school. (This study was undertaken at the request of the authorities at the Forest Hill School and the Royal Ontario Museum in an attempt to study a problem of practical educational concern to them.)

Subjects. Twenty children from each of three Grade 6 classrooms in Forest Hill Village, South Preparatory School, chosen on basis of being present for all lessons and tests. Groups A and B were considered ordinary class groups by the school. Group C was from a classroom considered to include "slower learners." On analysis of I.Q. however, it was found that for Groups A and B average C.A. was 11.2 months and I.Q. 121; Group C, 11.6 months, I.Q. 111.

Method. Museum trips included displays and objects, slides, illustration and maps, and a "project." Classroom procedure included written and pictorial forms (including maps). Two topics, the Aztecs of Mexico and the geology of Ontario, were used. The outlines followed were devised by the Museum staff, and were used in both settings. On the first topic Group A spent two afternoons at the museum while Group B learned the same material at school. On the second topic the groups were reversed. A test on the material was given the following day and again after three months. This included objective questions designed for simple scoring followed by one of an "essay type." Group C learned both topics at the museum and included during the period an elaborate project.

Results. The results were calculated from scores on items correct on the objective questions; and by judgments of independent judges on the essays at three levels—enumerative, descriptive, or interpretative (compare T.A.T. method). An item analysis of results on the objective questions was made. The means for each group were found and the reliability of their differences; this was done also for the various items making up the test. Types of responses on the essays were calculated as percentages.

Conclusions. 1. There is no significant difference between the total number of facts learned by the equivalent groups in the two settings. 2. The group of children of lower academic ability learn as much at the museum as the group of higher academic ability do in school on a picturesque topic such as the Aztecs. 3. The museum topics lead to essay answers which show more understanding, integration, and interest than are obtained from the topics learned at school.

T61. Thompson, Nina M. Investigation of the Change in I.Q. Occurring with Age Increase. 1948. Pp. 38.

Problem. To investigate the problem of I.Q. constancy, *(a)* by bringing together the accumulated research findings to date; *(b)* by analysis of a set of I.Q. scores obtained from one group of subjects over a period of 19 years.

Subjects. One hundred and eleven children ranging in age from 10 to 21 years who had been tested regularly as a part of a research study at the Institute. All subjects attended the Nursery School of the Institute at one time.

Material. 1. Findings regarding constancy of I.Q. included 26 studies. 2. Test scores for present study—515 between 2 and 6 years; 289 between 6 and 10 years; 230 over 10 years. Of these four is the minimum number given to any one individual and 100 individuals received at least seven. The tests used were Kuhlman test up to 4 years and the two revisions of the Stanford-Binet.

Results. 1. Research findings re I.Q. variation and possible factors related to variation are systematically reviewed and compared. 2. An analysis is made of the present set of test scores according to: *(a)* I.Q. distribution: (1) a gradual increase appears in scores at the upper age levels. (2) Correlation between first test and two tests, one at 10 years and one later, are .318 and .395. *(b)* Analysis of variation: spread is more extensive than that postulated by Terman. Variation is positive.

Conclusions. The variation in I.Q. scores revealed in this study is much greater than that expected or scientifically predicted. It is suggested by these findings that variation of I.Q. is to be expected. Factors used in other studies to explain I.Q. variation are not applicable to explain variation in the present study.

M17. NORTHWAY, MARY L., FRANKEL, ESTHER B., and POTASHIN, REVA. *Personality and Sociometric Status.* New York, Beacon House, Sociometry monograph no. 11. 1947. Pp. 73.

This includes (1) a review of the studies conducted at the Department of Psychology and Institute of Child Study prior to 1945; (2) paper on the social relationships of pre-school children by E. Frankel (see T55); (3) a sociometric study of children's friendships by Reva Potashin; this has had considerable influence on studies of children's social interaction now in progress; (4) a discussion of sociometry and some "challenging problems of social relations," and (5) instructions for using the sociometric test.

1948

T62. McLeod, H. N. A Rorschach Study with Pre-School Children. 1948. Pp. 46.

Problem. To investigate by the Rorschach test the hypothesis that a child's ability to think abstractly and to perceive with greater elaboration and differentiation increases with age between 4 and 6.

Subjects. Sixty children, 30 boys and 30 girls, ranging in age between 4 years 0 months and 6 years 11 months, attending the Institute Nursery School and Windy Ridge School. The range in M.A. was between 3–0 and 9–11.

Material. The Rorschach test.

Method. Analysis of Rorschach protocols obtained from the subjects using a standardized procedure of administration: Analysed *(a)* quantitatively, according to Location areas, and *(b)* qualitatively, according to (1) degree of accuracy, (2) number of responses, (3) rejections, (4) determinants, (5) content, and (6) populars.

Results. Quantitative analysis did not prove effective, but qualitative analysis showed C.A. and M.A. differences. These differences included: *(a)* decrease in personalization of perception; *(b)* increase in objectivity in terms of gearing perceptual experience closer to objective reality; *(c)* decrease in vagueness and a concomitant increase in elaboration and differentiation. Comparison of the results with those found by others in the field showed a high degree of agreement.

Conclusion. Rorschach findings demonstrate a development of the ability to think syncretically. This study can be used as a validation study, such norms enabling *(a)* the comparative assessment of the performance of the individual with others of his own M.A. and C.A.; *(b)* the validation of interpretive principles used at the adult level.

T63. Talbot, Betty M. A Longitudinal Study of Attentive Behaviour of a Group of Pre-School Children. 1948. Pp. 42.

Problem. To study developmentally the play behaviour of a group of pre-school children, with a view to clarifying characteristics of attentive behaviour, and arriving at an objective measure of attentive adjustment.

Subjects. Eleven children, 4 girls and 7 boys from the Institute's Nursery School. The age range was 2 years 4 months to 3 years 9 months. I.Q.'s ranged from 93 to 125.

Setting. The regular indoor play period in the Nursery School where normal playroom procedure was followed. The children were permitted free choice of toys. One adult supervised the playroom and controlled it with as little direction as possible. The number of children in the room varied from three to ten.

Method. Each child was observed for two 40-minute periods on three different occasions within a 16-month period. Observation was centred on the child's occupation with materials.

Recording. A judgment of behaviour was made at ten-second intervals. Behaviour was recorded by symbols according to the following categories: 1. In contact with material, *(a)* active use, *(b)* no physical use, *(c)* imaginative use, *(d)* routine activity. 2. Not in contact with material, *(a)* physical activity, *(b)* imaginative play, *(c)* passive. Materials used were recorded. Comparison between the four recorders showed 85 to 90 per cent accuracy.

Analysis of Data. Each series of two observations for each child was set up as a column diagram. The columns arranged from left to right showed the actual sequence of activity per category. The height of the column showed the duration of each unit in the sequence. These diagrams reveal individual differences and developmental change in pattern of attentive behaviour.

Results. 1. Group Tendencies: More than 50 per cent of time is spent in "active use" (1*a*). Median number of changes of activity per 40 minutes is 44; "active use" occurs with greatest frequency. Average length of units of "active use" is three times as long as for other categories (1½ min). Prolonged units of "active use" occur sporadically.

2. Developmental Trends: Total duration of "active use" tends to increase with age; "making no use of material" (1*b*) tends to decrease. Frequency of change of activity tends to decrease. Frequency of units of "active use" increases. Duration of units of "active use" increases while duration of units in which child makes no use of material or is passive decrease.

Summary. For the greater proportion of the play time the children actively use the play materials provided; this proportion increases with age. Interruptions are frequent but of shorter duration than the periods of activity and they tend to decrease in frequency and duration.

Conclusions. This study provides precise criteria for measuring attentive adjustment. Considering attention to be a fundamental factor in the development of activity patterns through play, these results then may be interpreted as revealing development in "purpose and concentration" or more broadly in "self-direction and self-control." According to the results for the particular children studied, development is towards greater self-direction and self-control, which is set forth as one of the aims of nursery school play activity programme. Whether this particular pattern of behaviour and developmental trend is typical of the pre-school child or a reflection of the particular nursery school system remains for further investigation. (B.M.T.)

T64. Yu, Hsi Chi. A Survey of the Parent Education Movement in the United States and Canada. 1948. Pp. 65+

Problem. To make a systematic study of the parent education movement in the United States of America and Canada under the following headings: 1. History of the development of the parent education movement in the United States of America and Canada 2. Leadership in parent education 3. Content of parent education 4. Methods of parent education with a view to introducing parent education into a community which hitherto has had no such programme.

Method. The sampling method is used. Contact with eighty-three organizations was made by correspondence and a study made of various published reports of parent education programmes and of literature. The material is presented in tables.

Results. 1. Parent education has come under the guidance of many types of organization, ranging from those specially set up to carry out parent education to a variety of government bodies. 2. The presentation of scientific information to parents and the public is being carried on by three types of persons—the specialist, the professional, and the lay leader, trained by various organizations in various ways. 3. The content of parent education as evidenced through a study of a random sampling of literature is highly varied. 4. Parent education methods in use are extremely varied and in each organization a number of methods are utilized.

Conclusion. The parent education movement in the United States of America and Canada is still in the formative stage. It has however developed certain characteristics and suggests certain broad principles of operation which can be applied in evolving a parent education programme in other countries.

T65. KARAL, PEARL. An Analysis of the Social Activities of Children Studied Developmentally. 1949. Pp. 49.

Problem. To analyse the social activities of a group of children in their out-of-school hours in order to determine the presence of developmental trends between 6 and 16 years.

Subjects. Forty-three children, 24 boys and 19 girls, graduates of the Institute Nursery School, who had passed their sixteenth birthday.

Material. The records of the Institute, more particularly those "follow-up" questionnaire forms filled in annually by parents only, when the children are younger, and by both parents and children later.

Method. The records were analysed under the general areas of: Family Life, Friends, Clubs, Recreation, Extra-curricular Studies, Visits to Relatives, Sunday Companions, and Sunday School.

These areas were evaluated according to the amount of weekly time they filled, and their incidence at successive age levels.

Results. 1. Relatively little available time was spent as and considered as "family time" throughout 2. Solitary activities predominated in recreation 3. The pressure of extra-curricular studies was intense, affecting 81 per cent of the group 4. There was increasing formalization and external organization of clubs 5. Visits to relatives, and Sunday School, did not figure largely in terms of frequency and time.

Conclusion. Group "trends" did not emerge as clear age differences; rather, trends consistent with each child's unique developmental pattern, were conspicuous. (P.K.)

1949

[T66. LAIDLAW, R. G. M. Studies in Security—II—an analysis of the method of evaluating test items in the area of "vocational" security of university students, 1949. Pp. 31.]

[T67. LAURENCE, MARY W. Studies in Security—I—a clarification of the concept in the familial area, 1949. Pp. 46.]

T68. STEE, MARJORIE J. An Investigation of Self and Family Identification by Pre-School Children. 1949. Pp. 51.

Problem. To investigate the concept of self in the pre-school child by measuring the child's ability to identify himself and the members of his family with paper dolls, and to verbalize the interrelationships.

Subjects. 146 normal children 2 to 5 years of age attending the Institute Nursery School; of these 50 children age 4, 31 boys, 19 girls; 50 children age 3, 25 boys, 25 girls; 46 children age 2, 23 boys, 23 girls.

Materials. Paper dolls made from poster cardboard, coloured, pleasant facial expression, numbered for purposes of recording, two dolls of each sex in every age group as follows: infants, pre-school age, school age, adolescents, adults, and older adults. A sample family of mother, father, pre-school age child, older brother, baby sister. Four animals were included: duck, bunny, cat, dog.

Method. Subjects were approached in Nursery School and brought to the testing room, which was familiar to the child. Each child was examined individually. Language used by experimenter was such that the pre-school child understood what he was required to do. Rapport was established chiefly en route and with the paper dolls which the children were allowed to handle freely. A sample family was presented and described to the child. The rest of the paper dolls were laid out in random order. Child was instructed to select himself and then his family. The following form of questioning was used: "Show me which one is you." "Which one is X?" (using child's name). "Now let's find your family." During the time of selecting family only three set questions were used: "Who is that?", "Who else is in your family?" "Who is Y?" When the child indicated he had selected his entire family, set questions were asked regarding relationships. A special form for recording was used. The method of measurement was a qualitative analysis.

Conclusions. Results showed that these pre-school children had the ability to select representatives of self and family members, and that there was a gradual increase in this ability with age, and an increase in the ability to select appropriate representations in regard to both age and sex, from 50 per cent adequacy at the two-year level to a high degree of accuracy at the four-year level.

Of the group, 58 per cent identified themselves as pre-school age, and 20 per cent as school age. Only 8 per cent identified themselves incorrectly as to sex, 3 per cent identified themselves as animals, and 7 per cent did not select a representation of self. *Only* children in this study identified themselves with their appropriate age group more often than did children with siblings.

Accurate selections included 90 per cent of the fathers, 80 per cent of the mothers and 67 per cent of the siblings. The two- and three-year-olds selected father more frequently than mother by 18 and 17 per cent respectively. At the four-year-level, both were selected almost equally. Most of the fatherless children selected a doll to represent father. A larger per cent of younger than older siblings were named and identified with paper dolls. Thirty-six of the children selected representatives of grandparents, aunts, and uncles. (Such relatives were not included in the sample family.)

Adequacy of response scores on interrelationship questions for the total group were as follows: self-parent relationship 80 per cent; sibling-parent relationship 90 per cent; self-sibling relationship 73 per cent; sibling-sibling relationship 40 per cent. There was a general increase on adequacy of response scores with increase in age on all the questions. (M.S.)

T69. THOMSON, MARY. An Analysis of the Sociometric Ratings of Groups of Children from Three to Eight Years of Age. 1949. Pp. 32.

Problem. To study the constancy of sociometric status measured at short intervals and to discover the characteristics of group constellations of children at nursery and primary school.

Subjects. Thirty-nine boys and 31 girls at Windy Ridge School from nursery school senior children to second grade.

Materials. A modified form of sociometric test using criteria satisfactory for the groups' age and situations.

Method. 1. The sociometric test was given to each child individually every week for four weeks and again after a three-week interval. 2. The scoring followed Bronfenbrenner's method—e.g. choices received related to chance expectancy. 3. The nursery, kindergarten, first grade, and second grade scores were each analysed as a unit.

Results. 1. The number of choices used by the children increased with age and practice. 2. The percentage of scores in each "chance interval" was much the same for all grades. In every group the largest percentage of scores fell in the interval "immediately below chance." 3. There were high positive correlations for all groups over all the intervals (in the +.6 to +.8 range); the correlations dropped slightly with increase of the interval and increased with the age of the group. 4. The amount of change in social status was calculated on the number of children whose status shifted from one level of chance expectancy to another. The actual changes were only 41 per cent of the possible changes. This percentage is almost the same among the four age groups. 5. Ninety-three per cent of all changes were between adjacent chance levels. Shifts between separated levels occurred only in the younger age groups. 6. Seventy-six per cent of the cases shifted no more than one level throughout the five tests. 7. A form of scatter diagram was made showing number of choices given and received by all subjects in one group on all five tests. From inspection of this choice patterns of children in this age group are recognisable. The typical pattern is that of each child selecting two or three children who have high preference value for him and scattering the rest of his choices casually through the group. These show that preference rather than chance predominates continually through the tests. 8. Sex cleavage was found throughout the age levels except the nursery school. 9. Reciprocal scores increased with age but were consistent from test to test.

Conclusions. 1. Children in the lower school grades present a picture on a sociometric test similar to that reported for older children in other studies, with the majority of scores falling below chance expectancy. Nursery school children approximate this picture except that their performance on the test itself is slightly poorer than that of older children, but skill in performance increases with practice.

2. There is a constancy in the group pattern of young children— even nursery school children—over a period of time. This constancy is more marked with older groups. As the time interval increases this group pattern changes slowly.

Nursery school and kindergarten children do not change their social status appreciably more often than grade children. In all groups the amount and degree of change is relatively small.

3. Most children of this age follow a fairly consistent pattern in making choices which can be assumed to reveal information about their social lives. Two or three children receive most of the choices from one child with the rest of his choices scattered throughout the group. Children tend to confine their choices to a relatively small proportion of the entire group, indicating selective factors. It may be assumed then that the average child of this age has two or three important friends who rate highly with him. There are variations of this general trend.

4. Children of this age tend to choose children of the same sex. This tendency increases from nursery school to second grade.

5. Mutual choices appear within all four age groups but they are more pre-dominant in the older groups. This would seem to indicate that there are more real "friendships" in second grade than at nursery school. These friendships are inclined to continue over a fairly long period (eight weeks).

1950

[T70. AINSWORTH, L. H. Rigidity as a Manifestation of Insecurity. 1950. Pp. 66.]

[T71. BLUM, MARY H. Studies in Security—X—Security of Adolescents in Their Use of Money. 1950. Pp. 64.]

T72. OLSTEAD, MARGERY. Performance on the Children's Form of the Rosenzweig Picture-Frustration Test as Related to Sociometric Status. 1950. Pp. 29.

Problem. To discover whether differences in sociometric status are related to differences in response to frustration as measured by the Rosenzweig test.

Subjects. One hundred and thirty-eight children (69 boys and 69 girls) in four classrooms of Grades 4 and 5 at the North Leaside schools. The age range was from 9 years, 6 months to 11 years, 5 months.

Apparatus. 1. An adaptation of Northway's form of the sociometric test. 2. The children's form of the Rosenzweig Picture-Frustration Test.

Method. 1. The sociometric tests and the P–F tests were given to each classroom group on the same day according to standard procedure. 2. The sociometric results were divided into three groups, A (24 cases) significantly above chance expectancy; B (84 cases) around chance expectancy; C (30 cases) significantly below chance expectancy. 3. Results on each of the 6 categories, 9 factors, 6 super-ego patterns and conformity ratings of the Rosenzweig P–F were computed for the three sociometric groups and measures of significance between the distributions calculated, (i.e. 66 comparisons). 4. C.R.'s of 3 or above are taken to mean *significant* differences, of 2 or above to indicate *trends*, below 2 *not markedly different*.

Results. 1. The detailed statistical results of the 66 differences on each measure of the Rosenzweig are given. 2. Of the 66 comparisons

only 20 showed any difference between the sociometric groups. Of
these, 8 were "significant" and 12 "trends"; thus two-thirds of the
items show no discrimination between children of varying social
status. 3. The interpretations of the items which do discriminate lead
to the following conclusions:

Conclusions and interpretation. Highly accepted children appear
to be less overwhelmed by frustrating situations than are those of
lesser or least acceptance. Perhaps this is because previous success
has made such children more confident in their own ability either to
handle the situation themselves, or to enlist the aid of someone else
on their behalf. In dealing with a frustrating situation, the highly
accepted child directs his aggressive feelings outwards and blames
other people and things rather than himself. It may be that realization
of his own popularity causes him to feel safe within his social group.
He is thus able to assert himself more strongly and to express his true
feelings when frustrating situations arise. Because of his popularity,
it is not necessary that he either find a solution for the frustrating
situation himself or that he wait passively for a solution to come his
way. Because of previous success, he is probably aware that he can
successfully demand that someone else solve the problem for him.

The child of low social acceptance is more readily blocked by
frustrating situations than the highly accepted child. Perhaps because
of previous failure in the solution of such situations, he has learned
that it is safer to gloss over the difficulty than to risk further failure.
He is inclined, therefore, to minimize the frustration almost to the
point of denying its presence and to absolve the "frustrating" individual. He is patient in the hope that the frustrating situation will
eventually be resolved.

The child of intermediate acceptance, like the child of low is more
readily blocked by the frustrating situation than is the "star." He is
inclined to minimize the frustration almost to the point of denying
its presence. However, he is more likely than either the "outsider" or
the "star" to view the situation as embarrassing because he has involved another person in his difficulty. Rather than blaming others for
the frustration or attempting to smooth over the difficulty, he accepts
the blame himself. Perhaps his reactions are indicative of a more
mature acceptance of responsibility and a greater tact and social
sensitivity than is evident in either of the other two sociometric levels.

In conclusion, the present author would like to postulate that the
reactions of the child of intermediate acceptance indicate certain

trends desirable from a mental hygiene standpoint. The "outsider" is apparently too socially insecure and afraid of failure to assert himself sufficiently. In the face of difficulty, he is patient and conforming. The "star" is perhaps so socially secure that it is unnecessary for him either to blame himself or to exhibit concern for others.

[T73. URQUHART, GERMAINE M. A Study of Negative Behaviour in Infants. 1950. Pp. 68.]

[T74. WALTER, ONALEE J. A Clarification of the Concept of Security in the Area of Competition. 1950. Pp. 47.]

[T75. WHITEHOUSE, B. M. Belongingness; Its Nature and Measurement. 1950. Pp. 41.]

T76. WISMER, RUTH E. A Survey of Individual Differences in the Paintings of Pre-School Children. 1950. Pp. 54.

Problem. To discover if there is a characteristic way of painting for the individual child, distinct from group tendencies or developmental trends; in order to compare the relative influence of learning and personality upon children's paintings.

Subjects. Twenty-two nursery school children (8 girls and 14 boys), who attended the Institute regularly over a three-year period.

Materials. The complete set of paintings completed by each of the 22 children during their attendance. The number of paintings per child ranged from 46 to 395, with a total for the group of 3164 paintings. Easels, uniform-sized paper, and the four primary colours, were provided, but the specific content was left entirely to the child.

Method. Analysis was carried out on the basis of formal elements that were defined. These elements were: (a) form used (line, mass, dot, and circle); (b) location of page used; (c) size of painting used; (d) colour used. Each child's attendance was divided into four equal parts, to allow comparative study of equal periods in the child's development.

Results. Individual patterns closely follow group patterns in (a) use of form; (b) extent of use of each area; (c) frequency of use of various fractions of the paper; and (d) use of colour.

In terms of the problem: (a) more consistencies than differences appeared in the use of the four elements; (b) developmental trends did not appear, since very few developmental changes were indicated.

Conclusions. 1. Group tendencies were more outstanding than individual differences. 2. A developmental sequence did not appear. These results may represent a preliminary stage before developmental changes begin, and further research with older children seemed indicated.

1951[10]

[T77. Davis, Inez A. A Study of the Adjustment of Children of the Same Families in Certain Routine Situations. 1950. Pp. 23.]

[T78. Campbell, Eleanor M. A Study of Differences in Interaction Patterns of Pairs of Children Chosen According to Sociometric Relationships. 1951. Pp. 60.]

[T79. Graham, Joyce R. P. A Study of Laughter as a Form of Interaction Between Children of Defined Sociometric Relationships. 1951. Pp. 40.]

[T80. Macnamara, Phoebe. Personality Scales: A Study in Methodology. 1951. Pp. 65.]

[T81. Miller, Charlotte H. A Study of the Social Interaction of Pre-School Children Paired According to Sociometric Ratings. 1951. Pp. 48.]

[T82. Karrys, Eva. A Comparison of Delinquents and Non-Delinquents on their Feeling of Security and Insecurity in the Familial Area. 1951. Pp. 72.]

[T82. Shirai, Tsune. Developmental variation in the visual discrimination of cube size by children two to thirteen years of age. Pp. 66.]

[10]These theses are not included in the review of the research.

Index

Index of Authors of Documents

(T = unpublished thesis; A = article; M = monograph; B = book.)